M000170288

THE WORD IS VERY NEAR YOU

WILFRID STINISSEN, O.C.D.

The Word Is
Very Near You

(Deuteronomy 30:14)

~

Translated by
Sister Clare Marie, O.C.D.

IGNATIUS PRESS   SAN FRANCISCO

Original Swedish edition:
Ordet är dig nära
© 1997 Libris, Örebro

Cover art:
Pantocrator
Private Collection, Madrid, Spain
© Album/Art Resource, New York

Cover design by Enrique J. Aguilar

© 2020 by Ignatius Press, San Francisco
All rights reserved
ISBN 978-1-62164-288-6 (PB)
ISBN 978-1-64229-120-9 (eBook)
Library of Congress Control Number 2020930373
Printed in the United States of America ∞

Contents

Contents

Preface

All Christian literature and preaching are actually nothing more than an attempt to explain and interpret what God himself has spoken to us. God is active in his Word, and, without any previous knowledge, a person can be affected by the power of the Bible's texts. But God is also active in man's research and seeking, in his stage of study and knowledge. "You search the Scriptures, because you think that in them you have eternal life; and it is they that bear witness to me", says Jesus to his opponents (Jn 5:39). And it is not because of this search that he later reproaches them, but because they did not seek in the right way and therefore did not come to know him.

In Jewish tradition, study of the Scriptures has always had a prominent place, and from her beginning, the Church has continued in the same path, above all through the Fathers of the Church. In our day, with its growing development of scholarly methods, exegetes have made immense progress in both Protestant and Catholic circles. Ecumenical cooperation has also gone considerably well for a long time in this area.

God's Word is one and the same, and different interpretations from different traditions cannot divide the Word itself.

Biblical scholarship is not my field, and I have felt

a certain hesitation to publish a work on this subject. But urged by my readers and listeners to do it, and in cooperation with a close friend, these six chapters have developed from different lectures I have given. My wish is only to give some simple instructions on how we can draw nearer to God's Word and let it penetrate us in order to let it bear fruit in our lives.

For those who are seeking a thorough account of biblical interpretation in the Church, I would warmly recommend the notable document, highly regarded in many Christian circles, that was published by the Pontifical Biblical Commission in 1993 ("The Interpretation of the Bible in the Church").

I have personally found much guidance for my Bible reading in the writings of Henri Cardinal de Lubac (who died in 1991). Chapter 2 in this book is in a special way inspired by his thoughts.

Bible reading and prayer belong inseparably together, and both are indispensable for anyone who wishes to live in close communion with God. If this little book can contribute to a deeper understanding of all the treasures that are hidden in the field of God's Word, it will be a joy for me. But without prayer, one's understanding will only be a superficial glitter that will soon disappear.

"Orent ut intellegant", Saint Augustine said: "May they pray so that they can understand!"

—Wilfrid Stinissen

On the Essence of the Bible

"For the word of God is living and active."
(Hebrews 4:12)

Divine Word

It belongs to God's being to be Word. God speaks unceasingly. "In the beginning was the Word, and the
Word was with God, and the Word was God" (Jn
1:1). God's Word is himself. It is his essence to go out
of himself. He is constant motion, incessantly flowing
water, relationship. His Word is his beloved Son. Life
is his own life.

It is in this Word that we are created, "for in him
all things were created, in heaven and on earth, visible and invisible, whether thrones or dominions or
principalities or authorities—all things were created
through him and for him" (Col 1:16). God speaks his
Word to me personally when he allows me to come
into existence. I exist because God continuously whis-
pers my name, says who I am.

My being is to be
A word from heaven
That speaks silently of love
And God's mystery.[1]

Since God speaks first, our first task is to listen. This listening is not something abstract but completely concrete. God has himself spoken in a concrete way in human language. His words are preserved; they are always accessible; we have them in our midst in the Bible. A Christian can see how the whole Bible is an interpretation of the only Word of God who is Christ the Son. On every page, it is him whom we meet. Even for those who do not know him, it is he who is the hidden one who reveals himself. He himself has said: "You search the Scriptures, because you think that in them you have eternal life; and it is they that bear witness to me" (Jn 5:39).

The Bible is not a book like any other book. It is not possible to compare the Bible with other books and say that it is better, wiser, truer. The Bible is something completely different. All other books give us human words. The Bible gives us God's Word.

The Second Vatican Council says unambiguously: "Those divinely revealed realities which are contained and presented in Sacred Scripture have been committed to writing under the inspiration of the Holy Spirit." Both the Old and the New Testaments are said to have

[1] *Livet är min vän* (Life is my friend). Meditative texts of a Carmelite nun (Tågarp, Glumslöv: Karmeliterna, 1992), p. 25.

been written under the inspiration of the Holy Spirit in their entirety and "have God as their author". "Everything asserted by the inspired authors or sacred writers must be held to be asserted by the Holy Spirit."[2] The Scriptures witness also about themselves: "All Scripture is inspired by God" (2 Tim 3:16). "No prophecy ever came by the impulse of man, but men moved by the Holy Spirit spoke from God" (2 Pet 1:21).

The Infinite in the Finite

How is it possible that an infinite, unlimited God expresses himself with finite, limited words? How can God speak "through men in human fashion"[3] without betraying himself? The human word clearly has an inner capacity beyond all expectation to express the eternal. The Word has this in common with all of the material creation. Matter can become the bearer of the divine, which is seen in the Incarnation. God becomes man, and in this man "the whole fulness of deity dwells bodily" (Col 2:9). We need not abandon Christ as man to meet him as God. No. "He who has seen me has seen the Father; how can you say, 'Show us the Father'?" (Jn 14:9).

The same is true of the sacraments. We do not need to search behind or beyond the material in order to find

[2] Vatican Council II, Dogmatic Constitution on Divine Revelation *Dei Verbum* (November 18, 1965; hereafter cited as *DV*), no. 11.

[3] Ibid., no. 12.

the spiritual reality. It is a question of seeking the divine in the human, the spirit in matter. There is an openness in matter that gives it the ability to receive and contain a spiritual power to be a channel for a divine reality. Oil that is blessed by the Church can become a bearer of the Spirit. That we do not notice it probably results from the fact that our spiritual senses are not especially developed.

God breaks through matter and lifts it far beyond its natural capacity. "It is", writes Hans Urs von Balthasar (1905–1988) "as if an oak tree were transplanted into a flower pot."[4] But, of course, the oak tree nevertheless does not destroy the flower pot, but, rather, the flower pot grows together with the oak without for that reason ceasing to be a normal flower pot. So also are those words that make up the Bible; completely normal, human words, but at the same time they are completely divine: they mediate a divine message.

We can enter at any time into a very concrete contact with God. We can at any time hear him speak to us. We need only to open the Bible and read. God speaks via these human, ordinary, almost commonplace words. When we listen to a recording of a person's speech, we hear only words that were spoken at one time but that no longer exist and, therefore, cannot bring about a living contact between the one who speaks and the one who listens. It is not that way when we listen to

[4] Hans Urs von Balthasar, *The Grain of Wheat: Aphorisms*, trans. Erasmo Leiva-Merikakis (San Francisco: Ignatius Press, 1995), p. 71.

God in the Scriptures. His Word is eternal. What he has once spoken, he speaks always. "For ever, O LORD, your word is firmly fixed in the heavens" (Ps 119:89). "The grass withers, the flower fades; but the word of our God will stand for ever" (Is 40:8).

Do we receive this treasure that God entrusts to us? He speaks to us in an eternal now, and each and every one who opens his Bible and his heart hears him speak. Perhaps we say that we believe this. It is possibly obvious to us, but if we do not often take time to read the Bible, we show that faith is not active in our lives.

To See the Bible in Its Whole Perspective

If God is actually the author of the Bible, the message that the Bible communicates must be true. Yes, it must be the definitive truth. It sounds extremely pretentious, but we can do nothing but admit that this is so. Access to the definitive truth belongs to the essence of Christianity. To distance oneself from this faith would be to offend God.

But having access to the truth is not the same as owning it. Often we do not allow the truth to enter in; we do not accept it, not enough anyway. The great claim of Christianity can hardly lead to pride or self-sufficiency. It leads sooner to a deep compunction of heart. The one who takes his Christian faith seriously cannot boast about what he is. He becomes, instead, very small since he sees ever more clearly that the truth he confesses is constantly obscured by his way of living.

When Christianity maintains that the Bible contains the definitive truth, it brings up questions. *Can* we really say that everything in the Old Testament is true? When the Psalmist complains: "You have put me in the depths of the Pit, in the regions dark and deep" (Ps 88:6, a psalm we pray in the Catholic Church every Friday evening), is it true, then, that the dead are separated from God?

The Second Vatican Council says: "Since Holy Scripture must be read and interpreted in the sacred spirit in which it was written, no less serious attention must be given to the content and unity of the whole of Scripture if the meaning of the sacred texts is to be correctly worked out. The living tradition of the whole Church must be taken into account along with the harmony which exists between elements of the faith."[5] Every single statement must be interpreted within the context of the entire message.

The Bible gives an account of salvation history.[6] The Bible is not a treatise about the essence of God and man, but a story of how God progressively reveals the truth about himself and man. He does not

[5] *DV* 12.

[6] "The Old Testament in fact presents a story of salvation, the powerful recital of which provides the substance of the profession of faith, liturgy and catechesis." Pontifical Biblical Commission, *The Interpretation of the Bible in the Church*, presented to Pope John Paul II, April 23, 1993.

say everything at once. Like a good teacher, he takes man where he is, and with endless patience he helps him to rise up gradually to a higher level.

He usually communicates just as much of himself as man is able to receive. If God had spoken to Israel from the beginning about his own inner life, his Trinitarian being, it would have been completely misunderstood and interpreted as vulgar polytheism. It was necessary that God first impress upon them that he is the One God and that there is no other. Only when that had taken root and become self-evident could it be meaningful to speak about three different Persons in God.

This is true also for ethics. Israel could not receive Jesus' New Commandment about love: "A new commandment I give to you, that you love one another; even as I have loved you" (Jn 13:34). When man is in his primitive, uneducated state, it is already much if he does not satisfy his desire for revenge. For him, the principle of retaliation: "an eye for an eye and a tooth for a tooth" is a great step forward. The conscience is trained successively.

The whole order of creation is marked by this progressive pattern of growth.

We often complain that God takes too long in revealing himself. We think that if he revealed a little more of his glory and his majesty, the world would look different. But those very people who have been able to behold something of God's glory admire his patience most and understand his method of teaching best. Saint Teresa of Avila (1515–1582) writes: "O my

Lord! . . . May the angels and all creatures praise You, for You . . . measure things in accordance with our weakness. . . . O Wealth of the poor, how admirably You know how to sustain souls! And without their seeing such great wealth, You show it to them little by little."[7]

God reveals himself in a historic process. The Bible's truth is a truth that gradually, progressively reveals itself. The Old Testament revelation is only a partial one that is directed toward the full revelation in the New Testament. In the words of the Second Vatican Council: "Now the books of the Old Testament, in accordance with the state of mankind before the time of salvation established by Christ, reveal to all men the knowledge of God and of man and the ways in which God, just and merciful, deals with men. These books, though they also contain some things which are incomplete and temporary, nevertheless show us true divine pedagogy."[8]

We do not say the same thing to a child as we do to an adult. Nor do we demand the same thing. Revelation has a dynamic development. The one who considers the Old Testament as something definitive without understanding that it receives its meaning from the New Testament must find that the Bible's truth is full

[7] Saint Teresa of Avila, *The Book of Her Life*, in vol. 1 of *The Collected Works of St. Teresa of Avila*, trans. Kieran Kavanaugh, O.C.D., and Otilio Rodriguez, O.C.D. (Washington, D.C.: Institute of Carmelite Studies, 1976), p. 263.

[8] *DV* 15.

of contradictions. There is no problem, however, for the one who has understood that salvation history is a long, growing process in which man gradually discovers God's truth and his own.

The Meaning of Life

The definitive truth is also the definitive meaning. To accept or reject the Bible is therefore a decisive matter. Man's destiny depends on it. If we reject the truth of the Bible, we reject life's genuine, original meaning. Since no one can live without meaning, we are forced to create an artificial meaning and live in illusions.

What does the Bible say concretely about the meaning of life? What is the Bible's fundamental message? I believe it can be summarized this way: "You, man, who think you are alone, are not alone. God exists, and he is God for you."

Martin Heidegger (1899–1978) speaks about *Geworfenheit* as one of the fundamental categories of the human condition. When man is not anchored in God, he has the impression of being thrown into existence and left there by himself. The one who does not flee from himself and seek his identity in work and achievement can hardly avoid perceiving a fundamental loneliness.

In reality, no one is interested in me. What really moves, drives, and inspires me leaves others indifferent. However much my friends assure me that they are not at all indifferent, that they are with me, there is still a disappointment that remains. Fundamentally, I am alone and uninteresting.

The Bible says no, you are not alone. You are not *geworfen* (outcast) but rather *geborgen* (protected). God is so interested in you that he is not content with giving you fine gifts. He comes where you are. He enters into your life.

The quintessence of God's Word is: I am with you, I am with you all. And the believers in the Bible are people who own this wisdom: The Lord is with us. The God of Israel is Yahweh (Jahve): I Am (with you). In the New Testament, he is Emmanuel: God with us. God is with his people.

For us, who are marked by an environment where God is completely silent, it is a good antidote to read the Bible and to be able to see in it that God is always there, how nothing happens outside of him, how everything that happens is an element in the love relationship with him. Jesus summarizes the whole Bible when, before he ascends to heaven, he says to his disciples: "I am with you always, to the close of the age" (Mt 28:20). And the Church repeats continuously in her liturgy: *Dominus vobiscum*, which can just as well mean the Lord *is* with you as the Lord *be* with you.

The Word that is with God and who is God becomes flesh, like you. He is interested in the very depths of your being. He gives up his own life for you. You are not uninteresting. You mean something to God. You are precious in his eyes. You are loved by him.

Therefore, it is also possible for you to exist for

others. The fact that God is there for you frees you from your prison, from the eternal rotation around yourself. He gives of himself, and we enter into his own centrifugal dynamic; a movement away from himself and toward others.

The one who truly lives with his Bible and learns there how God is *with* cannot do anything but be a person who is *with* others.

A Book of Unity and Reconciliation

That the Bible is God's Word does not at all mean that its message is foreign to the world or life. God does not speak to us so that we will turn away from what is earthly. His voice does not come to us from a sphere above the earth. We do not need to lift our eyes unceasingly to heaven. To the one who does so, the Bible says: "Why do you stand looking into heaven? This Jesus, who was taken up from you into heaven, will come in the same way as you saw him go into heaven" (Acts 1:11). The Bible is the great synthesis where everything becomes meaningful and everything receives its right place.

You do not need to leave the earth in order to reach me, says God. I myself come to you, I become earthly myself. You complain that you do not have time to seek me; that you must work. But I am myself in your work. I became a carpenter. You sigh that you are not spiritual enough to associate with me. But I have become matter, says God. And "from the rising of the sun to its setting" I take bread and wine and make it my Body and Blood. There is no conflict between spirit and matter, or if there once was such a contradiction, I, God, have conquered it.

The Bible proclaims the great atonement and that everything is definitively summed up in Christ (Eph 1:10).

What is original about the Bible and the Christian faith is that they do not emphasize God's transcendence so that man becomes less. The sense of God's greatness exists in the religiosity of the natural man. But the Bible continually emphasizes the greatness of man.

The concept of the person and the sense of the individual's value have deep biblical roots.

God respects man. He takes him seriously, makes him a dialogue partner, indeed, a covenant partner. The covenant bond is central throughout the whole Bible. It consists of the Old and the New Testament; that is, of two covenants. To make a covenant with someone expresses and means respect for the other. A master does not make a covenant with his slave; a father does not make a covenant with his child. A covenant presupposes a certain equality. Two married spouses bind themselves to a mutual surrender to each other. That is how it happens between people.

The incredible thing in the Bible's message is that the Creator makes a covenant with his creature and thereby gives him a dignity beyond anything we could imagine. "What is man that you are mindful of him, and the son of man that you care for him? Yet you have made him little less than the angels, and you have crowned him with glory and honor" (Ps 8:4–5).

It is difficult for man to believe in such a dignity. And as soon as he abandons God's Word, he also diminishes his self-respect. This is evident in our secularized time. Who believes in man's freedom, in his ability to take responsibility? Is everything not pre-determined by heredity and environment? The psychologist's primary task seems often to be to free man from guilt feelings without even clearly distinguishing if they are legitimate or unreasonable.

The Bible explains time and time again that man is free, that he can receive God's invitation to enter into a covenant with him or reject it. When God reacts so vehemently against the unbelief of Israel, it shows that he lets his people bear their responsibility. He does not explain sin away. He proclaims man's possibility to direct his life, to say yes or no to him. "See, I have set before you this day life and good, death and evil. . . . I call heaven and earth to witness against you this day, that I have set before you life and death, blessing and curse; therefore choose life, that you and your descendants may live" (Deut 30:15, 19). Man can choose. He is that great. To deny his freedom and responsibility is to limit and diminish him.

In the Bible, God and man are not competitors. God does not become less because man becomes greater. It is, on the contrary, man's greatness that reveals the greatness of God's love. Saint Paul cannot think of Israel's and our deliverance without breaking out into

a song of praise to God's *transcendence*. "O the depth of
the riches and wisdom and knowledge of God! How
unsearchable are . . . his ways!" (Rom 11:33).

Not Theories but Life

The Bible gives us a synthesis of the whole of reality,
but not, for that reason, a system. We do not find any
elaborate systematic theology or anthropology in the
Bible. It is always life that is primary. If you ask theoretical questions of the Bible, it will give you practical answers. You ask: Who is God? And the Bible
answers: Live life like a child of your heavenly Father,
dare to be a child, trusting and carefree; follow Jesus,
who is the image of the Father in the world, share
his sufferings and become like him in a death like his.
Wait on and listen to the Spirit, and let his fruit come
to full maturity in your life. You ask: What is prayer?
And the answer sounds urgent. This is how you shall
pray: Our Father . . .

What is love? It is wonderful to philosophize about
love, about eros and agape, but you have no time. Do
as the merciful Samaritan did, give food to the hungry.

Will many go to heaven or only a few, a majority
or a minority? "Strive", answers Jesus, "to enter by
the narrow door" (Lk 13:24). Do not waste time with
speculations about numbers, do not busy yourself with
statistics, but see to it that you get there.

God's revelation is called *law* by the Scriptures themselves. "Oh, how I love your law! It is my meditation

all the day" (Ps 119:97). What he communicates about
his being must be expressed in a new way of living.
Even the New Testament is a *law* that is at the same
time old and new. "Beloved, I am writing you no new
commandment, but an old commandment which you
had from the beginning; the old commandment is the
word which you have heard" (1 Jn 2:7–8).

It is not the philosopher who is the wise one in the
Scriptures but the one who keeps the law: "I understand more than the aged, for I keep your precepts"
(Ps 119:100). He who does not keep the law knows
nothing about God: "And by this we may be sure
that we know him, if we keep his commandments"
(1 Jn 2:3–4). "Do this," says Jesus, "and you will live"
(Lk 10:28).

The Scripture is also called the *way*, and it is a question of walking in it. "Blessed are those whose way
is blameless, who walk in the law of the LORD!" (Ps
119:1). Saint John the Baptist receives the call to prepare the way of the Lord in the desert (Mt 3:3), a way
on which God and his people can meet. Christians
are aware of having found this way, a way that is now
no longer only a law but a person, Jesus Christ. "I
am the way", he says (Jn 14:6). It is now a question
of walking in him (Col 2:6). And he himself says unceasingly: "Nevertheless I must go on my way today
and tomorrow and the day following; for it cannot
be that a prophet should perish away from Jerusalem"
(Lk 13:33).

What does all this mean? Simply that we cannot read

the Bible as just any other book. It is true that we can
read the Bible's law as a lawyer reads about legislation
of long ago or as an archivist reads a document from
an archive; but for a believer, Bible reading is something other than archeology. He knows that it is God
who speaks here and that his Word has an eternal dimension.

When now what God speaks is a law and a way, the
one who listens to God's Word cannot do anything
but obey that law and walk in that way. It belongs to
the meaning of the way that one should walk in it. And
only the one who sets out and begins to walk learns
to know the way. The first thing Jesus says when he
begins his preaching is: "The time is fulfilled, and the
kingdom of God is at hand; *repent*, and believe in the
gospel" (Mk 1:15, emphasis added). He does not begin
by explaining what he means by *God's kingdom*. Now
repent; that is, embark on a new way, the right way.
It is by the walking itself that we come to understand
what God's kingdom is.

For the one who hears God's Word, the walking is
the main thing. This is a criterion that gives us a possibility to judge our Bible reading. Does it lead to a
new life, or do we collect theoretical knowledge? Do
we allow ourselves to be affected by God's Word, or
do we keep enough distance so that we never come
into the danger zone?

Here we also have a criterion that can help us to
choose between different study circles about the Bible.

If we wish to be a part of a Bible study group, we

ought first to find out if the study is mostly about theoretical questions that actually have nothing to do with the Bible as it was intended by God. Only when the question has in it, at least in a latent way: "What do we do with this?" can the study be fruitful. We do an injustice to the Bible when we transform it into an object of discussion. It is meaningless to study and search out a way when we never wish to try it.

This is immensely important and can never be emphasized enough. Among those very ones who professionally dedicate much time to the Bible, there are many who are completely closed to the actual message of the Bible. We can give so much time and energy to technical details that we no longer see the forest for the trees, in other words, that the meaning itself which God is speaking to man is lost. The exegete runs perhaps a greater risk than others. His scholarly attitude results in a certain distance that stands in opposition to the immediateness that is necessary for God's Word to be able to bear fruit. If the Bible is only an uninteresting object of study for exegetes and does not concern him as a person and constantly question his existential values anew, it does him harm rather than good.

"It is necessary", said Pope John Paul II in a speech about the interpretation of the Bible in the Church, "that the exegete himself perceive the divine word in the texts. He can do this only if his intellectual work is sustained by a vigorous spiritual life. . . . Scientific study of the merely human aspects of the texts can make the exegete forget that the word of God invites each person to come out of himself to live in faith and love."[9]

> We are fortunately [writes Thomas Merton (1915–
> 1968)], living in an age of theological ferment and of
> Biblical renewal. All of us—scholars, simple believers
> or mere interested readers—stand in immense debt to
> the specialists who have done so much to really open
> the Bible to us. Nevertheless, in all the thousands of
> pages of Biblical scholarship that have been printed
> in the last hundred years we must admit, and anyone
> well read in the field must agree, that a high propor-
> tion of it is an arid, exhausting desert of futile de-
> tail which wearies the mind by distracting it from the
> meaning of the Bible and goes wandering aimlessly
> through a wilderness of technicalities where all inter-
> est withers and expires. Good Biblical scholarship is
> essential for a serious understanding of the Bible, but
> this scientific itch for arid and pointless investigations
> which throw no new light on anything whatever has
> deadened our sensitivity to the existential reality of
> Biblical experience.[10]

To Surrender to God's Word

The division that befell the Western Church at the
end of the twelfth century between theoretical theo-

[9] Address of Pope John Paul II on *The Interpretation of the Bible
in the Church*, April 23, 1993, no. 9.
[10] *Opening the Bible* (Collegeville, Minn.: Liturgical Press, 1986),
pp. 34–35.

logy and the contemplative and mystical tradition of wisdom is especially dramatic when it comes to understanding God's Word. Since God's Word is not only instruction, not even primarily, but above all a liberating message and transforming power, it cannot of course be understood from a merely scientific position. Saint Paul writes to the Thessalonians, who have listened to God's Word in his preaching, "And we also thank God constantly for this, that when you received the word of God which you heard from us, you accepted it not as the word of men but as what it really is, the word of God, which is at work in you believers" (1 Thess 2:13). This power of God can only work when man defenselessly surrenders himself to it, which is something completely different from an intellectual interest.

To surrender oneself to the Bible's message also means to refrain from presumptuously being selective regarding its content. If we choose certain passages that we especially like and leave out others that we find difficult to understand, we will never reach the whole truth. It is just this kind of selective reading that has given rise to sects and heresy. A sect is almost always built upon a partial truth that in a biased way overshadows the other complementary truths. The result is a picture of reality that is askew.

The whole Bible must be received with all its apparent contradictions. God's Word must be allowed to remain there, in all of its breadth and boundlessness. Since God is *coincidentia oppositorum* (the unity of opposites, Nicolaus Cusanus, 1401–1464), it is not strange that his Word often seems contradictory. It is impossible to express all at once the multiple aspects that coincide in him. As soon as God begins to speak with human words, he can do nothing more than place the emphasis on first one and then another aspect of his being. The one statement complements and even corrects the other. If we become fixed too much on certain assertions or claims, we get an incomplete and, therefore, a false picture of God. With a one-sided reading, we can prove almost anything at all by the Bible. It is vitally important for a Christian to read it without preconceived ideas, in total openness.

The one who thinks he already knows who and how God is beforehand will continually think he sees his idea confirmed when he reads the Bible. He reads his Bible with glasses that only let in those texts that correspond with his conviction. He simply does not see the other texts.

If you are convinced that God is some kind of policeman who is out to catch us in the act, a strict judge, then we would be at great risk of noticing only those texts that correspond to our understanding. God becomes all the more strict and cruel. "Truly, I say to you, you will never get out till you have paid the last penny" (Mt 5:26). "And cast the worthless servant into the outer darkness, where there will be weeping and gnashing of teeth" (Mt 25:30). "But I say to you that every one who is angry with his brother shall be liable to judgment; whoever insults his brother shall be liable to the council, and whoever says 'You fool!' shall be liable to the hell of fire" (Mt 5:22). All the wonderful texts of God's gentleness and mercy you skip over or do not understand that they could be for you.

In our day, there is perhaps a greater risk to overlook the texts that have to do with God's wrath and punishment and focus only on statements about his love. God can then easily become a good-natured, smiling uncle who turns a blind eye and gladly gives us an encouraging slap on the back. But God's love is something different from kindness or sentimentality. Everything the Bible says about God's wrath is necessary so that we will understand that his love has a serious, dramatic side and that our freedom to say yes or no to it is both a wonderful privilege and a terrible responsibility.

To surrender oneself to the Bible means to repeat again and again the question: "God, who are you?" There is more to know about God than what you now know. God is always greater. Even if I know that God is love, which is true, I still do not know what love is. "The love of Christ . . . surpasses knowledge" (Eph 3:19). I still do not understand "the breadth and length and height and depth" (Eph 3:18).

We should not interpret shocking verses in the Bible too quickly in the light of certain ideas we have about God. Perhaps it is just meant to be that my ideas about God are shaken. If I still do not understand, it does not matter. The Word must be able to remain in its full power. My perplexity does not give me the right to take the edge off of God's Word. It is not the Bible that should adjust to me, but it is I who should adjust to it. If even our relationship with other people should be marked by a deep respect because we can never completely understand the mystery of another person, how much more ought our attitude toward God and his Word be marked by a holy reverence! "Behold, God is great, and we know him not; the number of his years is unsearchable" (Job 36:26).

He is too high not only for our understanding but also for our will and our heart. God's plans for us surpass everything that we can yearn for ourselves. God's will is greater than what we are capable of accomplishing right now. Even in this respect, it is important to be without prejudice. "What is your will for me?" is always what we ought to ask when we read the Bible. The answer to that question always goes beyond our own limitations. God wants to do more than what you think you can do now; he enables you continuously to step over new thresholds, to go "from one degree of glory to another" (2 Cor 3:18).

It is no small plan that God has for mankind!

2

The Relationship between the Old and the New Testaments

"They were written down for our instruction."
(1 Corinthians 10:11)

It is tempting to set the Old Testament against the New and claim that since the New Testament contains the full and definitive revelation, the Old Testament no longer has any value for us.

It is true that it is in the New Testament and only there that God reveals himself fully and completely. The mystery that has been hidden is revealed in the Person of Jesus (Col 1:26). But the mystery was already there. The life that God breathed into man on the morning of creation was from the beginning a participation in the life of God's only begotten Son, for "in him all things were created, in heaven and on earth, visible and invisible, whether thrones or dominions or principalities or authorities—all things were created through him and for him. He is before all things, and in him all things hold together" (Col 1:16–17).

In the New Covenant, "when the time had fully

come, God sent forth his Son, born of woman, born
under the law" (Gal 4:4), this life has come forth in
visible form. "The life was made manifest, and we
saw it, and testify to it, and proclaim to you the eternal life which was with the Father and was made manifest to us" (1 Jn 1:2). But since the true life, Jesus
Christ himself, existed from the beginning in God's
creative-salvific work, still hidden in the Old Testament, it has an irreplaceable value for us Christians.
The Second Vatican Council says that: "The plan of
salvation foretold by the sacred authors, recounted and
explained by them, is found as the true word of God
in the books of the Old Testament: these books, therefore, written under divine inspiration, remain perma-
nently valuable", and refers to Saint Paul: " 'For all
that was written for our instruction, so that by stead-
fastness and the encouragement of the Scriptures we
might have hope' [Rom 15:4]. . . . These same books,
then, give expression to a lively sense of God, contain
a store of sublime teachings about God, sound wisdom
about human life, and a wonderful treasury of prayers,
and in them the mystery of our salvation is present
in a hidden way. Christians should receive them with
reverence."[1]

How Does Jesus See the Old Testament?

In the Gospel of John, Jesus says; "You search the
Scriptures, because you think that in them you have

[1] *DV* 14–15.

eternal life; and it is they that bear witness to me" (5:39). Everything that is said in the Old Testament is a mysterious and hidden witness about Jesus. He says further: "If you believed Moses, you would believe me, for he wrote of me" (5:46). The one who honestly seeks God comes to realize that everything to which the Old Testament refers has its fulfillment in Jesus, and he will eventually also come to recognize Jesus everywhere in the Old Testament. When Jesus reads the Old Testament, he cannot but constantly meet and recognize himself in these texts. Abraham's sacrifice on Mount Moriah surely helps Jesus to think of his own death. When at the Last Supper he sings praises, Psalms 113–18, with his disciples, he finds that in them his own attitude and feelings formulated as his life's mission are about to be accomplished.

After his Resurrection, Jesus accompanies the two distressed disciples on the way to Emmaus. He reproaches them for their slowness to understand all that the prophets said about the Messiah. "And beginning with Moses and all the prophets, he interpreted to them in all the Scriptures the things concerning himself" (Lk 24:27).

He could have proved his identity as Messiah by reminding them about how he had himself foretold his death and his Resurrection. Instead, he shows how he can fulfill expectations of the Old Covenant promise. In this way, he allows the disciples to understand the continuity in God's plan and how he himself is the one to whom everything points from the very beginning. It is not something completely new that finally makes man and the Word into what they are created to be. God's plan is realized by the fact that the old is integrated and explained in the new.

In the Sermon on the Mount, Jesus reassures: "Do not think that I have come to abolish the law and the prophets; I have come not to abolish them but to fulfil them" (Mt 5:17). Nothing of the old is rejected; on the contrary, Jesus confirms it by giving it a deeper meaning. The one who has met him and so learned to know God's innermost secrets can no longer content himself with dutiful faithfulness, fulfilling of concrete, defined commands. Communion with Jesus makes all the borders fall away: love must be absolute.

When Jesus says: "You have heard that it was said to the men of old. . . . But I say to you" (Mt 5:21–22), he does not contradict Scripture in order to come with something new. He goes to the bottom of what was said and draws out its actual and innermost purpose. His repeated: "But I say to you" is an explanation and a clarification of the old. In him the whole truth is revealed, the truth that in the Old Testament exists as a flower in seed.

The New Is Born of the Old

We can naturally read the New Testament by itself, but much is lost if we do not see it against the background of the Old Testament. Since Jesus did not come to nullify the Old Testament but rather to fulfill it, it is diffi-

cult to understand him if we do not know *what* he fulfills. Therefore, it is wise to follow the pedagogy that
he himself used when he instructed the disciples on the
way to Emmaus and go through the whole Old Testament in order to discover how it speaks about him.

The Old Testament opens itself completely only for
the one who sees it in relationship to the New. "The
New Testament lies hidden in the Old, and the Old
Testament lies open in the New", writes Saint Augustine (A.D. 354–430).[2]

However much we know about the people of the
Old Testament, of the history of Israel's development,
ritual prescriptions, and traditions, it still does not
mean that we *understand* the Bible. It is only the light
of Christ that can enlighten us. "If you want to understand, you can only do so through the Gospel", writes
Origen (ca. A.D. 182–254).[3]

The Gospel is the key to understanding the Old
Testament. To read the Old Testament as a whole in
itself goes against its own essence. Christians have always read the Old Testament on the basis of Christ
with their eyes on him. At Sunday Mass, the first reading is usually taken from the Old Testament. It re-
sponds, then, to the third reading, which is always from
the Gospels. The third gives the key to the first. The

[2] "Novum in Vetere latet, Vetus in Novo patet." *Quaest in Hept.*
2,73 (*PL* 34:623).
[3] Quoted in Henri de Lubac, *Medieval Exegesis*, vol. 1, "The
Four Senses of Scripture", trans. Mark Sebanc (Grand Rapids,
Mich.: Eerdmans, 1998), p. x.

Gospel itself also appears, then, in a new light when it stands out against its Old Testament background.

For a Christian, it is just as wrong not to read the Old Testament as it is to read it exclusively for its own sake. We can only reach a thorough understanding of the Old Testament if we see it as a mother who carries the new in her womb and brings it to birth.

Christ was present in the Old Testament, but incognito. For a Christian, that incognito disappears, and the secret of the Old Testament is revealed.

The books of the Old Covenant speak all the time about Christ. No one says it so clearly and in such a condensed way as Saint John in the prologue to his Gospel: "In the beginning was the Word. . . . And the Word became flesh and dwelt among us" (1:1, 14). That Word is Christ himself. Jesus identifies with the Divine Word, which according to the creation account created the world and which many times and in many ways spoke in times past to the fathers through the prophets (Heb 1:1).

God *is* Word. That is why the Word resounds in everything he creates. But the Word was concentrated when he spoke to Abraham, Isaac, Jacob, and all the people of Israel. The Word became even more concentrated and was received in an ever greater density until it finally became flesh in Jesus Christ. The Word bears a name, it is a Person. There is no longer a place in the Bible where we do not meet Christ. The *Catechism of the Catholic Church* quotes Saint Augustine when it writes "You recall that one and the same Word of

God extends throughout Scripture, that it is one and the same Utterance that resounds in the mouths of all the sacred writers, since he who was in the beginning God with God has no need of separate syllables."[4]

Just as we in our lives ought constantly to remind ourselves of our origin, that we exist here and now by God's creative Word, so we also ought to allow ourselves to be led by the Spirit back to the origin of the Word in our Bible reading, to that place where the Word was pronounced before it was written down. And that place is the Father who sends the Word, his Son, to be the light and life of man. When I read the Bible, both the Old and the New Testaments, I hear the Father speak to me, and what he speaks is the Word, Jesus Christ.

When the *Catechism of the Catholic Church* wishes to speak about the Bible, it begins with this heading. "Christ—The Unique Word of Sacred Scripture".[5]

The New Testament is born from the Old, without ever denying its mother. Mother and daughter are completely directed toward each other. The New Testament does not destroy the Old but, rather, fulfills, renews, and brings it to life. The letter of the Old Testament is transformed into Spirit by the New Testament. For a Christian reader who seeks only the

[4] *Catechism of the Catholic Church*, 2d. ed. (Libreria Editrice Vaticana; Washington, D.C.: United States Catholic Conference, 1997; hereafter cited as *CCC*), p. 30, quoting *Enarr. in Psalmos* 103, 4, 1 (*PL* 37:1378).

[5] *CCC* 101.

literal meaning in the Old Testament, Saint Paul's words apply: "For the written code kills, but the Spirit gives life" (2 Cor 3:6). For a believing Christian, the Old Testament exists primarily in its relationship to the New. The Old Testament is now understood by him *after* the Spirit has come, which means, not that the new understanding denies the old, but that it refuses to let itself be reduced to that.

This total transformation of the Old Testament is not the result of a slow development. It happens in an instant. It is true that it happens after a long preparation, but the transition is a shock. Suddenly there is a new register on the organ, and everything sounds different. This transition is the decisive, critical moment when eternity enters into time. From that moment, we live in the fullness of time. Previously mankind reached out toward the future; from this moment on, all hope, everything, is concentrated in the eternal now of Jesus Christ. Before we lived in the shadow, now we live in the fullness of truth. *Umbram fugat veritas noctem lux eliminat* (the truth dispels the shadow; the light drives away the night).[6]

*Christ Is the One Who Opens the Book
(cf. Revelation 5:5)*

As was said before, there is a continuity between the Old and New Testaments. The coming of Jesus is pre-

[6] From the sequence *Lauda Sion Salvatorem*, which is usually sung in the Catholic Liturgy on the Solemnity of Corpus Christi.

pared over centuries. Nothing is improvised. The Old Testament was like a sketch, a model in clay that showed how the golden vessel of the New Testament would look.

The New Testament is the fruit that grows on the tree whose roots, trunk, and leaves are the Old Testament. It is through the law that we come to the Gospels.

At the same time, a radical distinction exists. The New Testament is not like the Old. God's people are no longer limited to one single ethnic group. God's presence is no longer localized in one particular place, the tent of the Presence or the temple. Henceforth God is present everywhere in Jesus Christ.

The Old Testament itself proclaims that the new shall be completely different. "Behold, the days are coming . . ." (Jer 31:31–33).

The conversion from the letter to the spirit is so radical that it can only be explained as an anticipation of him who is Alpha and Omega, the first and the last (Rev 1:8, 17).

The entire history of the Bible strives and develops toward Christ. He is the driving force that starts the development and leads it and at the same time is the goal of the development. He is Lord of the prophets and the one who fulfills the prophecies. It is he who constitutes the unity of Scripture, since all of Scripture speaks about him. He is the only exegete of Scripture.

When we ask: "What or who is the Spirit of the law?" the answer is: Jesus Christ. He is the Logos of Scripture (meaning, significance, interpretation). He interprets the Scriptures, not primarily by what he says, but by who he is. He is the exegete of Scripture, not so much in word, but by action. Long before Jesus explains for the disciples on the road to Emmaus how the Old Testament witnesses to him, he has already interpreted it through his own life and his whole divinity and humanity. The images of the Old Testament and the prophets become clear and revealed when we see how they are fulfilled and realized in Jesus.

This exegesis begins already at the moment of the Incarnation. But it happens above all on the Cross when Jesus offers himself there. It is there, on the Cross, that he can say: "Behold, I make all things new" (Rev 21:5). There he kills the letter and *gives birth* to the Spirit.

The great transformation is carried out on the Cross. When he says: "It is finished", the Scriptures are fulfilled and everything that was hidden in them is revealed. His Cross is the key that opens all the books of the Old Testament. When he dies, he opens the book with its seven seals (Rev 5:5) and the curtain in the temple is torn in two, that which hid all the mysteries of grace. The book with God's mysterious plan now lies open, and everyone who wishes to read it can.

By fulfilling the Scriptures, Jesus gives them their true, deep meaning. Certain Church Fathers have compared this transformation to the transformation of the Eucharist. The Scriptures are like bread, but this bread is made nourishing and life-giving only by Jesus. To read the Old Testament without seeing that it speaks about Christ in its entirety is like receiving Communion before the Consecration.

The Church has always held unshakably fast to this unity between the Old and the New Testaments and rejected the idea that the Old Testament is something completely past along with the one who thinks that it should be revived and carried out according to the letter. The Old Testament can become a New Testament, not historically or chronologically, but by a completely new understanding of it.

The whole traditional Christian interpretation of the Bible is marked by a constant, flowing joy over this wonderful harmony between the Old and the New Testaments. We admire the harmony between both Testaments; we savor it, enjoy it. We compare it to beautiful music that surpasses the sphere of a heavenly concert.

We think that the new law is woven with the yarn of the old law. We compare the cord that joins the Old and New Testaments with the bond of marriage. That is why we can never separate the one from the other.

Saint Augustine goes still farther when he writes: "Lex spiritualiter intellecta Evangelium est" (the law understood spiritually is the Gospel).

The Gospels themselves give us two symbols to which the ancient Fathers of the Church return again and again and that, according to them, illuminate the relationship between the Old and the New Testaments. The first symbol is Jesus' Transfiguration. Together with

Jesus, Moses and Elijah appear. The Old Testament bears witness to the New. The clothing of Moses and Elijah are white like the clothes of Jesus. That means that the glory of the New Testament shines over the Old. But when the three disciples look around, there is no one but Jesus alone. The New Testament has absorbed the Old. That is why Peter makes a mistake when he wishes to build three booths. One single booth is enough since the law and the prophets are taken up into the Gospels.

The other symbol we find in the account of the miracle at Cana, when Jesus transforms the water of the letter into the wine of the Spirit.

The Psalms give us additional symbols. For example, Psalm 42:8. Just as deep calls to deep, so both Testaments call to each other, and the more we sound their depths, the more loudly their call resounds. One Church Father thinks of our two eyes that work together in order to see an object more clearly. So both Testaments also see one and the same object, they taste one and the same thing.

The Old Testament is a mysterious land where we continually discover roads that lead to Christ.

Continuity and Distinction in Synthesis

It is the Spirit's special gift to the Church from her very beginnings and to every individual Christian that enables us to see how the New Testament both fulfills and surpasses the Old Testament. In the Catholic

Church document on the interpretation of the Bible (1993) we read:

"It is in the light of the events of Easter that the authors of the New Testament read anew the Scriptures of the Old. The Holy Spirit, sent by the glorified Christ . . . , led them to discover the spiritual sense. While this meant that they came to stress more than ever the prophetic value of the Old Testament, it also had the effect of relativizing very considerably its value as a system of salvation."[7] If we read the Church Fathers and their commentaries on the Scriptures, we are often surprised by the fact that they contradict each other and even themselves. Sometimes they allow the Old and the New Testaments to contrast with each other, and sometimes they unite the Old and New Testaments so that they almost blend together. These apparent contradictions are understood first when we consider them as an element in a dialectic process that consists of a thesis and a synthesis that annuls the thesis, and a synthesis that unites and reconciles both. It is in this process that the Christian understanding of the Bible has received an ever clearer form.

The thesis says that the Old Testament is rich and fruitful because it paves the way for the New Testament. The Old Testament is an indispensable introduction and preparation for the New, a long, drawn-out birth process. As long as Christ has not come, the Old Testament is full of promises and budding life.

[7] Pontifical Biblical Commission, *The Interpretation of the Bible in the Church* (March 18, 1994), III, A, 2.

The antithesis maintains that the Old Testament loses its value when Christ comes. Yes, even that it can be dangerous, since we can so easily get stuck in it. To be fixed on the prophecy about the coming reality when the reality has come is like looking for the child in its mother's womb when it is already born.

The synthesis is: The Old Testament is still valuable, indeed, even more valuable than before Christ came, because we now understand it fully in the light of Christ. Only a Christian understands the Old Testament and can then also place a value on it and revere it.

He understands that Jesus is the *finis perficiens, non interficiens* of the Old Testament. The end that completes and fulfills, not the end that passes away, as Saint Augustine says.[8] The Old Testament does not die when the New begins. It finds itself again, but is now transformed, explained; exactly as the development to adulthood does not mean the death of childhood but, rather, its transformation.

To read the Old Testament without meeting Christ there could be called, in psychological language, a fixation, remaining at an earlier stage of development or regression, going back to an earlier stage. Ever since Christ opened the book, the mystery of the Old Testament has no longer been veiled. Not wanting to see the revealed mystery, that is to say, him, is the same as not wanting to grow.

[8] *In Johannem* 55, 2; CCL 36:464.

In Christ, the whole Bible finds its unity because everything in it is moving toward him. Christ makes one word out of all the words that are in the Scripture; God's Word. The Incarnate Word has often been called in tradition *Verbum abbreviatum*, the condensed word. In him all the words of the Bible are gathered together. Jesus himself indicates that he is *Verbum abbreviatum* when he says: "You search the Scriptures, because you think that in them you have eternal life; and it is they that bear witness to me; yet you refuse to come to me that you may have life" (Jn 5:39–40). What a tragic misunderstanding! The Pharisees are so eager to read the Scriptures and refer to them that they do not see that they are encountering the synthesis of the entire Scriptures.

Because a Christian in the Spirit understands all the biblical words' definitive meaning, he discovers their unity. The final meaning of all the words is Christ. All that the Law and the Prophets spoke of are gathered together in him. The Word that was born in Bethlehem of the Virgin Mary is the same Word of which the prophets spoke in the Old Covenant. It happened in another form but under the same influence of the Spirit.

The Church Fathers readily quote Psalm 62:11, "Semel locutus est Deus." God has spoken once; God speaks only one word, the Son, the Word that gives meaning to all words that speak about him. It is in him and only in him that everything becomes understandable.

"Christ, the Son of God made man," says the *Catechism of the Catholic Church*, "is the Father's one, perfect, and unsurpassable Word. In him he has said everything; there will be no other word than this one."[9] And the *Catechism* quotes the famous text by Saint John of the Cross (1542–1591): "In giving us His Son, His only Word (for He possesses no other), He spoke everything to us at once in this sole Word—and He has no more to say . . . because what He spoke before to the prophets in parts, He has now spoken all at once by giving us the All Who is His Son. . . . Any person questioning God or desiring some vision or revelation would be guilty not only of foolish behavior but also of offending Him, by not fixing his eyes entirely on Christ and by living with the desire for some other novelty."[10]

Christ in the Old Testament

When we read the Old Testament, the essential thing is that we meet Christ there, that we discover how everything points to him. "All of holy Scripture is one and the same book," writes Hugh of St. Victor (d. 1141), "and this only book is Christ, for all of holy Scripture speaks about Christ, and all of holy Scripture is

[9] *CCC* 65, p. 22.

[10] *Ascent of Mt. Carmel*, bk. 2, chap. 22, 3–5, in *The Collected Works of St. John of the Cross*, trans. Kieran Kavanaugh, O.C.D., and Otilio Rodriguez, O.C.D. (Washington, D.C.: Institute of Carmelite Studies, 1979), pp. 179–80.

fulfilled in Christ."[11] We cannot understand Scripture without seeing Christ in it, just as we cannot understand Christ and faith in him without understanding and believing in Scripture.

The one who reads the Bible with an open mind can hardly avoid seeing that Jesus is the completion and fullness of what was already foretold in the Old Testament. For the one who, so to speak, has discovered him, it can be like a game to try to find him everywhere in persons and events in the Old Covenant. There seems to be a connection between the New and Old Testaments that is like an inexhaustible spring. Some examples can cast light on this.

That Adam points to Christ we find already in Saint Paul: " 'The first man Adam became a living soul'; the last Adam became a life-giving spirit" (1 Cor 15:45).

Adam is an imperfect first sketch of Christ. Adam is created in God's image, but Christ is God's image. This relation to Christ is left even after Adam's Fall. The deepest reality in him, that he is created in God's image, is not destroyed by the Fall. In an indirect way, we receive even from the first chapter of the Bible the comfort that even fallen man has a likeness to Christ. Something in him is untouched by sin. Our whole earthly life is a pilgrimage, a search to find our full identity in that which was not ruined by sin.

The Letter to the Hebrews sees a connection between Abel and Christ. Both were murdered, and the

---

[11] *De arca Noe morali* II, 8 (*PL* 176:642CD).

blood of both cries to heaven. But while Abel's blood calls out for punishment for Cain (Gen 4:10), the blood of Christ cries out more strongly: it cries out for God's mercy and forgiveness (Heb 12:24).

We can perceive Christ in Noah when he is saved from the flood of sin. This is not a gratuitous, capricious invention of a lively imagination, but it is the New Testament itself that recognizes Christ in Noah: "who formerly did not obey, when God's patience waited in the days of Noah, during the building of the ark, in which a few, that is, eight persons, were saved through water. Baptism, which corresponds to this, now saves you, not as a removal of dirt from the body but as an appeal to God for a clear conscience, through the resurrection of Jesus Christ" (1 Pet 3:20–21).

Abraham is a magnificent prototype of Christ. Just as he hears that he shall leave his land and his father's house (Gen 12:1), so Jesus leaves his Father's house, his Father's bosom, in order to become one of us.

Isaac, who according to God's command shall be sacrificed (Gen 22:1–13), points clearly to Jesus. But what in Isaac's case only indicates and gives a sketch becomes with Christ deadly serious.

The fight of Jacob with God (Gen 32:24–30) is an image of the struggle that Jesus has in Gethsemane with his Father.

Moses is himself conscious that he prefigures Christ: "The LORD your God will raise up for you a prophet like me from among you, from your brethren—him you shall heed" (Deut 18:15). When Peter gives his speech after having healed the lame man by the Beautiful Gate, he says explicitly that this prophet is Jesus (Acts 3:22).

David, as king, bears the title of the Anointed One, which in the Vulgate is translated as Christus. For the one who, for example, reads Psalm 18:51: "faciens misericordiam christo suo David" (he shows mercy toward David his anointed), the very words lead one's thoughts to Christ. David is chosen by God and points as such to him of whom the Father speaks: "And a voice came out of the cloud, saying, 'This is my Son, my Chosen; listen to him!' " (Lk 9:35).

But David is far from being free from sin. As a sinner, he is surely not similar to Christ. Yes, Jesus has taken upon himself the sin of all mankind. And Jesus makes the words of David in the Psalms his own and lets them formulate his own prayer. He feels no need to sort out certain penitential psalms that express contrition and anguish. He recognizes himself in them all. He is the Lamb of God who bears and takes away the sin of the world.

"Let us therefore recognise in Him our words," writes Saint Augustine, "and His words in us: Nor when anything is said of our Lord Jesus Christ, especially in prophecy, implying a degree of humility below the dignity of God, let us hesitate to ascribe it to Him who did not hesitate to join Himself unto us."[12]

---

[12] *Enarr. In Psalmos* 86, 1; CCL 39, 1176; *Nicene and Post-Nicene Fathers*, 1st series, vol. 8 (Peabody, Mass.: Hendrickson, 1995), p. 410.

That Jesus is present everywhere in the Old Testament coincides with a well-known text by Saint Melito, bishop of Sardis (d. before A.D. 190) that is from the Office of Readings for Holy Thursday in the Catholic Liturgy of the Hours:

"It is he who endured every kind of suffering in all those who foreshadowed him. In Abel he was slain, in Isaac bound, in Jacob exiled, in Joseph sold, in Moses exposed to die. He was sacrificed in the Passover lamb, persecuted in David, dishonored in the prophets." [13]

[13] *Hom. in Pascha* 2, 7, 69 (*SC* 123:99); from an Easter homily by Saint Melito of Sardis, in Office of Readings for Thursday in Holy Week, *The Liturgy of the Hours*, vol. 2 (New York: Catholic Book Pub., 1976), p. 459.

3

Spiritual Interpretation of the Bible

"And we impart this in words not taught by human wisdom but taught by the Spirit, interpreting spiritual truths to those who possess the Spirit."
(1 Corinthians 2:13)

To read the Bible in order to learn something about Israel's history or to read it in order to meet Christ there, what a difference!

Pray in Order to Understand

One ought always to begin Bible reading with a prayer that in that Word of God we will meet Jesus Christ. If we do not meet him, we miss the essential. "Why do you not devote your free time to reading the Scriptures?" writes Saint Ambrosius (ca. 340–397). "Do you not occupy yourself with Christ? Why do you not speak with him? Why do you not listen to him? By reading the Scriptures, we listen to Christ."[1]

[1] *De officiis ministrorum* I, 20, 88 (*PL* 16:50A).

The life of a Christian is completely Trinitarian. That is why our Bible reading ought to have a Trinitarian stamp. We listen to the Father who speaks his Word, Jesus Christ, and we receive it and try to understand it in the light of the Spirit, enlightened by him. He is the Spirit of truth who leads us into the whole truth, that is to say, Jesus Christ.

It is wise to begin the reading of the Bible with a prayer that expresses just this Trinitarian dimension, for example, the following:

"God, Father of heavenly light, you have sent your Son, the Word who became flesh, to the world in order to reveal yourself to us men. Pour out your Spirit over me now so that in that Word which comes from you I may meet Jesus Christ, learn to know him in a deeper way, come to love him with an ever greater love, and then come to the blessedness of your kingdom, Amen."[2] When we open our Bible, we are like the blind and need to pray: "Lord, let me receive my sight" (Lk 18:41). Before we begin to praise God in the morning, we usually say: "Lord, open my lips." We ought also to say: "Lord, open my eyes and my heart" before we begin our Bible reading.

Just as the Consecration (the transformation at the Eucharist) presupposes the *epiclesis* (the prayer by which the Church asks the Holy Spirit to transform the bread and wine into the Body and Blood of Christ), so also our Bible study presupposes an epiclesis: it is the Spirit

[2] Enzo Bianchi, *God ontomoeten in zijn Woord* (Bonheiden: Bethlehem Abbey, 1991), p. 89.

who makes these lifeless letters into God's living Word and teaches us to recognize everywhere him who is our life, Christ. We can be certain that this prayer is heard, for the Father in heaven desires nothing more than to give the Holy Spirit to those who ask him (Lk 11:13).

The Holy Spirit was not only there when the Bible texts were written down through inspiration. He is also there when we read these texts, presupposing that we have an open heart and a willing mind. His presence guarantees that the text never becomes old but retains an eternal youthfulness.

If one's Bible reading is to bear fruit, the text must be constantly *actualized and personalized*. The text was, to be sure, written a long time ago, but since it is God's Word and everything that belongs to God has an eternal dimension, it is still very real and present. God speaks it today. The most important thing now is not how Israel or the Pharisees reacted to God's Word, but how I react. How do *I* receive God's Word that is directed to *me* today? Does the seed fall in good soil, or does it fall by the wayside?

The Fourfold Meaning of Scripture

According to an old tradition, which is also mentioned in the *Catechism of the Catholic Church*, we can distinguish between two different senses or types of significance: the literal and the spiritual. It is later further categorized in allegorical, moral, and anagogical significance.

A medieval verse summarizes these four senses:

> The Letter speaks of deeds; Allegory to faith
> The Moral how to act; Anagogy our destiny.[3]

The *literal* sense is what the author had in mind when he wrote the text. This meaning is the fundamental one, and the spiritual sense is as a rule supported by it. It is often enough to hold to the literal sense in order for the text to have a concrete meaning in life. For example:

> "As a deer longs for flowing streams, so longs my soul
>   for you, O God" (Ps 42:1).

> "As for me, I am poor and needy . . . do not delay,
>   O my God!" (Ps 40:17).

Even when we read: "The earth is full of the mercy of the LORD" (Ps 33:5), we can really mean it. Thanks to our faith, we have the ability to see God's glory right through all sin and cruelty.

The historical accounts of the people of Israel read according to their literal sense teach us much about God's educating, forming, and unfailing faithfulness, that he is always there in the midst of the concrete history of mankind.

But the meaning of the Bible text is not limited to what the author meant when he wrote it. It has a *spiritual* sense, a deeper dimension that becomes accessible only if we read the text with an openness to God's

---

[3] "Littera gest docet, quid credas allegoria, moralis quid agas, quo tendas anagogia." Augustinus of Dacia, *Rotulus pugillaris*, I, ed. A. Walz: *Angelicum* 6 (1929): 256, cited in *CCC* 118.

Spirit. This deeper meaning is not something that is put into the text but, according to the encyclical *Divino afflante Spiritu* (1943), is actually in the text. It is for us to discover it.

1. The *allegorical* sense is the most important in the spiritual interpretation. It is a deeper, more thorough meaning that is hidden in the text and that explains how everything points to Christ. What distinguishes the Bible from all other books is not only that its words represent a reality, but that the represented reality in its turn refers to an additional reality that has to do with Jesus and his work of redemption.

"Thus the crossing of the Red Sea", says the *Catechism*, "is a sign or type of Christ's victory and also of Christian Baptism."[4] Saint Paul writes: "All were baptized into Moses in the cloud and in the sea" (1 Cor 10:2). The allegory is the mystery that is revealed in history. And the mystery is eternal and present.

Just as the Eucharist is not only a memorial service of what Jesus did once but also is a celebration where his sacrifice becomes real and present, so also is God's Word an eternal, living Word that speaks *now*, that communicates God's thought and love *now*. For the one who is only interested in historical facts without seeing that they point to a deeper reality, God has no possibility of conveying what he wishes to say. But for the one who is sensitive and always waiting for something more, the Word becomes living and active.[5]

[4] *CCC* 117.
[5] "The empirical facts as such have no interest for the believer except for their religious import. . . . Christian 'allegory,' as

The allegory is not only in the Old Testament's references to the New Covenant in Christ. Even many New Testament texts have a deep dimension that cannot always be read in a literal way. According to Saint John, all of Jesus' miracles are *signs* of a divine message. All episodes in Jesus' life and suffering reveal something of God's inner life and disposition.

We can, for example, reflect on why Jesus keeps silent when the high priest Caiaphas asks him: "Have you no answer to make? What is it that these men testify against you?" (Mt 26:62–63). His silence is a direct *exeges* (explanation) of God.

When man wishes to force God to speak, when he wants to manipulate him or besiege him, he keeps silent. God answers our foolish, egotistical questions with silence. He does not solve our problems with detailed explanations. For the one who has the courage to endure God's silence, it eventually gives in itself all necessary answers.

If God always gave direct answers, we would never cease asking irrelevant questions. God's silence makes us realize that much of that questioning and wonder-

---

opposed to that of the Greeks, is not an imaginary account, a coherent set of metaphors. It is indeed a history, not simply as an account of exterior episodes, but as the uncovering/unveiling of their hidden significance; it is the 'truth of salvation' which it contains and which Scripture reveals." Ignace de la Potterie, "Reading Holy Scripture 'in the Spirit': Is the Patristic Way of Reading the Bible Still Possible Today?" *Communio* 13.4 (Winter 1986): 314–15.

ing is meaningless because it shows a lack of trust and surrender.

The Old Testament points to Jesus, and Jesus himself points to the Father. Or, more correctly, to the Trinity. Even when it is a question of the New Testament, we can speak of a spiritual meaning. When Jesus cries out: "My God, my God, why have you forsaken me?" (Mk 15:34), he reveals not only the world turning away from God but also the endless spaces and abysses that exist within the Trinity between the divine Persons. A word like: "I and the Father are one" (Jn 10:30), however, allows us to realize something of the equally incomprehensible closeness that exists between them.[6]

One can even say that Christ's being itself reveals the mystery of the Trinity. "Christ's essence is itself trinitarian."[7] By the fact that he unites the divine and human nature in the unity of his Person, he shows the distance that exists between the Father and the Son and how it is conquered in an independent Person, in the unity of the Holy Spirit.

Jesus lives unceasingly through the Spirit, in relation to the Father. If we come to know Jesus and listen to him, we cannot but be reminded of this.

2. The *moral* and *tropological* (*tropos* means way of acting) meaning tells us how we are to act. The Scripture

[6] Hans Urs von Balthasar, *The Grain of Wheat: Aphorisms*, trans. Erasmo Leiva-Merikakis (San Francisco: Ignatius Press, 1995), p. 72.

[7] Ibid., p. 62.

text must give rise to a new way of acting. "Now these things happened to them as a warning, but they were written down for our instruction", says Saint Paul (1 Cor 10:11). The moral interpretation means to see how we shall *translate the truth of the faith into daily life.*

The anagogical or eschatological meaning points to the goal of our strivings, heaven. It lifts up, *anagô*, our gaze and allows us to anticipate eternal life. So the Church on earth is an image of the heavenly Jerusalem.

3. Medieval authors gladly point out the relationship between the threefold spiritual meaning and the three theological virtues: faith, hope, and love. The allegorical meaning corresponds to love: What shall we believe? The moral corresponds to love: What shall we do, and how shall we act? And the anagogical meaning relates to hope: Where are we going?

Henri de Lubac (1896–1991) has four threads in his great work *Exégèse médiévale: Les quatre sens de l'Écriture.*[8] He emphasizes that it is extremely important to respect the order of the threefold spiritual meaning and that the moral must always come *after* the allegorical. To begin with, we should try to understand what the events recounted in Scripture mean for our faith. Only then can we see what this entails for our actions. If we go the opposite way, we risk reducing Christianity to moralism, when in reality it is a message about God's love.

---

[8] Published in 4 vols. (Paris: Montaigne, 1959–1964). Three vols. have been translated into English by Marc Sebanc and E. M. Macierowski as *Medieval Exegesis* (Grand Rapids, Mich.: Eerdmans, 1998–2009).

The Bible gives us the pattern for the whole Christian life. Mysticism and ethics belong inseparably together but must always stand in the right order. Our actions become empty if they do not come forth from communion with Christ. "Apart from me you can do nothing" (Jn 15:5). It is the one who first comes to him, hears his word, and then acts who builds his house on solid ground (Lk 6:47–48).

The Spiritual Meaning Comes from the Spirit

Saint Thomas Aquinas (1225–1274) writes that the author of the biblical text is an imperfect instrument in God's hands. What he speaks of he understands *cum aliquo cognitionis defectu*, with defective, imperfect knowledge. "Sometimes the person whose mind is moved to utter certain words", he writes, "knows not what the Holy Ghost means by them."[9] The Holy Spirit means much more than what the author realizes.

The spiritual meaning is just as inspired as the literal. Every authentic meaning is just as inspired as the literal. As long as we have not penetrated into the deeper levels, we have not understood so much of the Spirit's meaning. And still, however deep we may go, there are always deeper levels to reach. The Scriptures, because they are God's eternal Word, have an eternal dimension. There is always more to discover. Saint Gregory

[9] *Summa Theologiae*, II-II, q. 173, a. 4, trans. Fathers of the English Dominican Province, vol. 2 (New York: Benziger Brothers, 1947), p. 1905.

(ca. 540–604) likens the Scriptures to the four creatures in Ezekiel that go straight forward in the four
directions of the compass (1:12). Just as God does not
create the universe once and for all but continuously,
so the Spirit also creates continuously. And as space becomes ever greater by the fact that the galaxies move
away from each other, so all Scripture becomes greater,
at least for the one who reads with faith. In the same
measure that faith is deepened, the Scriptures also expand. In understanding the Scriptures, we can say what
Saint Augustine maintains about God: "Si finisti, Deus
non est" (If you have understood, it is not God).[10]

The spiritual meaning does not lie outside the literal. It is not a little appendage. The spiritual meaning
ought never to be sought *beyond* the literal but always
within it, just as we do not find the Father beyond the
Son, but rather in and through him. The Word has
become flesh: in the flesh we must meet the Word in
the God-man. The Spirit's eternal, unlimited thought
is incarnated in a limited human word.

Many present-day theologians devote themselves primarily to positive knowledge. This is not wrong. Such
knowledge is necessary in order to expose the literal
meaning in the Bible, that which the author intended.
Since the spiritual meaning is hidden in the literal, we
do not come to the spiritual without first having discovered the literal. Nor is it wrong for there to be an
effective distribution of work. Everyone does not need

[10] Saint Augustine, *Sermo* 53, 12 (*PL* 38:370).

to do all. The ideal would, of course, be for exegetes and theologians to be spiritual people. What is essential, nevertheless, is for the one who devotes himself to scholarly exegesis to be conscious of the fact that this is only a part of the exegesis and that the integral exegesis also tries to give answers to the question: What does God mean by the Word of Scripture?

The truly great exegetes have always known that the historical research, to which they are forced to limit themselves for practical reasons, is not the whole exegesis.

Some Examples

We can illustrate the teaching about the literal and the spiritual meaning with a few examples. The meaning is not, of course, that with every reading of the Scripture we should systematically look for this fourfold meaning, but, rather, only to show that a word of Scripture is an unexpectedly rich land that is worth researching.

1. Manna. The literal meaning is that the people of Israel who were about to starve in the desert discover one morning that there is "a fine, flake-like thing, fine as hoarfrost", that is eventually called manna (Ex 16:14, 31). God has given them something to satisfy their hunger. According to the allegorical interpretation by Saint Paul and Jesus himself, the manna is an image of the heavenly bread. "And all ate the same supernatural food", writes Saint Paul (1 Cor 10:3). And

Jesus says to the people: "It was not Moses who gave you the bread from heaven; my Father gives you the true bread from heaven" (Jn 6:32). This bread from heaven is both God's Word and the Eucharist.

The moral meaning is naturally that we should live by God's Word and receive the Eucharist. Jesus himself says: "Truly, truly, I say to you, unless you eat the flesh of the Son of man and drink his blood, you have no life in you" (Jn 6:53). We should live Eucharistically.

The anagogical or eschatological meaning teaches us that the Eucharist is our food for the journey on the way to heaven and "a pledge of our future glory", as Saint Thomas Aquinas says in the well-known prayer *O sacrum convivium*. "To him who conquers I will give some of the hidden manna, and I will give him a white stone, with a new name written on the stone which no one knows except him who receives it" (2:17), we read in the Book of Revelation. That is, we shall live from the life of Christ through all eternity; he shall be our actual, true life.

2. The bronze serpent. According to the letter of the text, Israel had become afflicted with poisonous snakes in the desert as a punishment for their rebellion against God.

At his command, "Moses made a bronze serpent, and set it up as a sign; and if a serpent bit any man, he would look at the bronze serpent and live" (Num 21:9).

If we only kept to the literal meaning, we would perhaps raise our eyebrows. The episode does not seem to be free from elements of magic.

It is primarily the allegorical meaning that gives us the key to understanding. Jesus himself reveals this meaning in the conversation with Nicodemus. "And as Moses lifted up the serpent in the wilderness, so must the Son of man be lifted up, that whoever believes in him may have eternal life" (Jn 3:14–15). The footnote in the Swedish translation explains that the words lifted up imply in part that Jesus shall hang upon the Cross and also that through his suffering he will be raised up to God and be glorified.

The *moral* meaning is that we shall look on Jesus who heals our wounds. "Therefore, holy brethren, who share in a heavenly call, consider Jesus, the apostle and high priest of our confession", says the Letter to the Hebrews (3:1), and: "looking to Jesus the pioneer and perfecter of our faith, who for the joy that was set before him endured the cross, despising the shame, and is seated at the right hand of the throne of God" (12:2).

The *anagogical* meaning we find expressed in a wonderful way in Saint Paul: "Therefore God has highly exalted him and bestowed on him the name which is above every name, that at the name of Jesus every knee should bow, in heaven and on earth and under the earth, and every tongue confess that Jesus Christ is Lord, to the glory of God the Father" (Phil 2:9–11).

3. The prophet Jonah. According to the *literal* meaning, Jonah is punished because of his disobedience. He does not want to set out to Nineveh and admonish the people to conversion. He is swallowed by a great fish and is three days and three nights in the belly of the whale (Jon 1:17).

Jesus himself explains the *allegorical* meaning of the story: "For as Jonah was three days and three nights in the belly of the whale, so will the Son of man be three days and three nights in the heart of the earth" (Mt 12:40). The striking and literal meaning of the hardly credible story about Jonah we understand only when we see it in the light of Jesus' death and Resurrection. In this light, it becomes extremely significant. The sign of Jonah is the great, indeed, the only sign that Jesus gives to his people. "An evil and adulterous generation seeks for a sign; but no sign shall be given to it except the sign of the prophet Jonah" (Mt 12:39).

The moral meaning is that we, like Jesus, cannot rise to new life if we are not prepared to die. We cannot be fruitful unless we, like the grain of wheat, first fall to the ground and die—the law of the grain of wheat (Jn 12:24). For Saint John of the Cross, Jonah's stay in the belly of the whale is an excellent image of the dark night.

> Since the divine extreme strikes in order to renew the soul and divinize it (by stripping it of the habitual affections and properties of the old man to which the soul is strongly united, attached, and conformed), it so disentangles and dissolves the spiritual substance

—absorbing it in a profound darkness—that the soul at the sight of its miseries feels that it is melting away and being undone by a cruel spiritual death. It feels as if it were swallowed by a beast and being digested in the dark belly, and it suffers an anguish comparable to Jonas's when in the belly of the whale [Jon. 2:1–3]. It is fitting that the soul be in this sepulcher of dark death in order that it attain the spiritual resurrection for which it hopes.[11]

If we see the story of Jonah in an *eschatological* light, we can consider life on earth as a life of darkness. As long as we remain on this earth, we live in the darkness of faith. We know about the light, but we do not see it. The earth is a "valley of tears", while at the same time we are aware that we are on the way to "the eternal light". Bodily death is then no longer so frightening but, rather, a crossing over from darkness to light. "I am not dying, I am entering into Life", says Saint Thérèse of Lisieux (1873–1897).

4. The wedding feast at Cana. According to the *letter* (the literal meaning), Jesus comes to the aid of the newly wedded couple in an embarrassing situation: they run out of wine in the middle of the wedding feast (Jn 2:1–11).

That this miracle is an *allegory*, a sign, Saint John says himself: "This, the first of his signs, Jesus did at Cana

[11] Saint John of the Cross, *The Dark Night of the Soul*, II, 6, 1, in *The Collected Works of St. John of the Cross*, trans. Kieran Kavanaugh, O.C.D., and Otilio Rodriguez, O.C.D. (Washington, D.C.: Institute of Carmelite Studies, 1979), p. 337.

in Galilee, and manifested his glory; and his disciples believed in him" (Jn 2:11). This first sign that casts light on all that follows shows that the Christian life is a wedding feast where Jesus is the true Bridegroom. It is he who is the actual host. He who offers wine. The Mother of Jesus is also there and plays an important role at the feast.

The *moral* meaning is manifold. We can consider Christian life as a feast and live in joy. We ought to be conscious of the fact that our relationship to Jesus is that of a bride and bridegroom. Our love for him ought to claim all our energies. We ought to understand that we may not overlook Mary in our life. We can also learn that there ought to be a crescendo, an intensification in our life. In God's kingdom, the good wine comes after the wine of lesser quality. When one gets older, he loses his physical strength, he becomes tired and worn out. But for the spiritual man, life becomes ever more beautiful and rich (2 Cor 4:16).

The anagogical meaning leads our thoughts to the heavenly wedding hall. "The kingdom of heaven may be compared to a king who gave a marriage feast for his son" (Mt 22:2). "Let us rejoice and exult and give him the glory, for the marriage of the Lamb has come, and his Bride has made herself ready. . . . Blessed are those who are invited to the marriage supper of the Lamb" (Rev 19:7, 9). The wedding at Cana is an image of the heavenly wedding feast where the Bridegroom himself serves his guests. "Blessed are those servants whom the master finds awake when he comes, truly, I say to you, he will put on his apron and have them sit at table, and he will come and serve them" (Lk 12:37).

The Meaning of the Words of Scripture in the Liturgy

In her liturgy, the Church reads the whole of Scripture in relation to the mystery of Christ. She does it with an endless flexibility. The meaning can change according to the liturgical season in which we find ourselves or the feast that is celebrated.

So, for example, Jerusalem becomes either the Church or the heavenly Jerusalem. When the Psalms speak about the sun that rises from the end of the heavens and its circuit, which is to the end of them (Ps 19:6), the Church, inspired by Saint Paul (Rom 10:18), can think of the preaching that reaches out over all the earth. Psalm 19 has often been called *apostolus* because it is always used on the feasts of the apostles.

The temple, the holy place, the house of the Lord, or tent is the Church or the glorified Christ or intimate companionship with him. The death we fear is an image of eternal death: to be separated from Christ. Life, on the other hand, is the fullness of life lived in communion with him.

To go up to Jerusalem is a symbol of the Christian life, which is about going up to the heavenly Jerusalem hand in hand with Jesus. When we pray that the Lord be lifted up, we think of Christ being lifted up on the

Cross (Jn 12:32) or of his Resurrection and Ascension.

Israel has been able to see our inheritance of sonship; that we in Christ are children of the Father. When the Old Testament speaks about marriage, we think of a wedding between Christ and the Church. When we read: "By the waters of Babylon, there we sat down and wept, when we remembered Zion" (Ps 137:1), we are reminded of sin and its consequences. That we live in estrangement, far away from the Lord.

The sinner, the godless, or the evil mockers who accuse and persecute us and to whom the Psalmist reacts with atrocious curses are the power of evil within us or in the world. If we interpret these curses this way, in their spiritual, genuine meaning, they become a prayer full of confidence; we pray that God will make manifest these evil powers that try to destroy his work in us. Or it is also the Lord himself who speaks these words in his fight against the powers of darkness.

Saint Benedict (ca. 480–547) had no problem with these vengeance psalms in Scripture. When he says that we shall seize the devil's temptations while they are small and crush them against Christ, he is naturally inspired by Psalm 137, which speaks about Babylon, the destroyer. "Happy shall he be who takes your little ones and dashes them against the rock!" (Ps 137:9).[12]

---

[12] *The Rule of St. Benedict*, Prologue 28.

Babylon is the power of evil for Benedict, and Babylon's children are none other than the evil thoughts and desires that the Evil One stirs up in our hearts. The one who loves Christ hates everything that will kill his life in us and in others; just as God hates the sin because he loves the sinner.

Gregory of Nyssa (ca. 330–394) interprets the verse from Ecclesiastes: "A time to love, and a time to hate" (3:8). We love Christ, and therefore we hate everything that opposes him.

For the monks of old, and not only for them, it was natural to interpret the vengeance psalms in this way. They did not remain in the literal sense but knew that all of Scripture had to do with Christ: "He is before all things, and in him all things hold together" (Col 1:17). That is why they did not feel the need to leave out such psalms from the liturgy, either. They prayed the entire Psalter without any problem.

This whole perspective is no longer obvious in our time. We need to learn to see how everything is an image of and points to a deeper reality. It is faith that gives us the deeper vision. In principle, Baptism has opened our eyes. For us it is about practicing this ability that we have latent within us.

The Playful Interpretation

There is yet another way to interpret the Scriptures, namely, the playful interpretation where we seek, or rather find, completely new personal meanings.[13] We can be like children and play with the text and come to completely unexpected, original interpretations, suited to our own particular situation.

To a certain degree, we can read the Scriptures in the same way that we read poetry. Obviously, in reading, we should always take the content of faith, that is to say, the whole context, into consideration. But within that context there are limitless possibilities of constantly seeing new facets.

It is typical of poetry, just as for art, that it appeals to the reader's or the beholder's creativity. A poem is not a treatise where the thoughts are already thought through and have received their final formulation. A poem opens a door, often many doors at the same time, and the reader decides himself which path he chooses or how long he wishes to walk on it. It is, among other things, this combination of guidance and freedom that makes us feel at home in the land of poetry. We feel respected and taken seriously. We may then interpret and associate ourselves, be ourselves a co-creator.

This is also true of our contact with God's Word, which has an extensiveness and a multiplicity of meanings that merely human words cannot cover. As a free child of God, I may play in the paradise of the Bible. I may make the old text into a *new song* that corresponds with my own personal experience, my actual

[13] See Pirmin Hugger O.S.B., *Ein Psalmenlied dem Herrn* (Munsterschwarzach: Vier-Turme-Verlag, 1980), pp. 40–46: Beten im Spielsinn.

needs. I can be sure that God enjoys this way of playing with the text: "Then I was beside him, like a master workman; and I was daily his delight, rejoicing before him always" (Prov 8:30). When I do so, I unite myself with the Church's centuries-long tradition. The Church Fathers have read the Scriptures in this way, and the Church does it in her official liturgy. It is truly not psychoanalysis that has discovered this free association. The Church makes use of it with immense virtuosity.

A few examples from the Church Fathers. When Saint Augustine reads the words "A warrior's sharp arrows, with glowing coals of the broom tree" (v. 4) in Psalm 120, he associates it with cupid, *amor*, the Roman god of love that pierces the heart with his arrows of love. In reality, the warrior's sharp arrows are about God's punishment that afflicts the liars with betraying tongues. But Saint Augustine does not care about this. For him, it is about arrows of love: "The warrior's sharp arrows are God's Word", he writes. "When they are shot, they penetrate our hearts. And when our hearts are pierced by God's arrows, we are not annihilated but rather ignited with love."[14]

When the dead boy in Shu'nem rises to life again after the prophet Elijah has laid on him, he sneezes seven times (2 Kings 4:35). Saint Bernard of Clairvaux (1090–1153) explains why the boy sneezes just seven times. He is an image of the Church. When she

[14] *Enarr. in Psalmos*, 120, 4.

is raised to life by Jesus, she opens her mouth seven times in order to carry out her sevenfold daily hymn of praise, according to Psalm 119:164: "Seven times a day I praise you."[15]

In his commentary on the Book of Deuteronomy, Origen speaks about departure from Egypt and the long period of wandering in the desert. Israel is released from Egypt and goes through the desert and different enemy territories in forty-two stages. This wandering through the desert is, for Origen, a spiritual wandering that has its designated stations. At every stopping place, an inner development occurs, a deepening of the relationship with God. The different territory names that the Bible mentions give us the key to understanding what happens at every station according to Origen. "Why should we refuse to believe that these territory names mark the progress that the students make in the study of the divine?"[16]

Origen compares this long development with another enumeration, but now in the New Testament; namely, the genealogy of Jesus in the Gospel of Matthew. The list of Jesus' forefathers includes three groups of fourteen names; that is forty-two in all. Just as God's people must wander to the Promised Land in forty-two stages, so Jesus steps down to us in forty-two stages and helps us to go the same way until we reach the Father.

---

[15] *In Canticum*, sermon 16, 3.
[16] *Hom. In 4 Mos*, 27, 13.

In his playful contact with the Scriptures, Origen is no beginner. His sophisticated commentaries, about the forty-two steps, bear witness to a mastery in the genre. Our play with the text will probably have more humble proportions.

A playful interpretation that we meet again and again in the spiritual tradition is the Psalm verse: "*Deep calls to deep*" (Ps 42:7). In the text, it is about the sound of the rapids' undulating, swelling waves. But as the text is formulated, it gives an exceptional way of expressing man's insatiable desire for God. Two eternities meet each other. There is hardly a mystic who has not recognized and expressed his longing for God in this psalm verse.

We are truly in good company when in this playful way we interact with the Scriptures. Saint Augustine does not call his commentaries on the Psalms *exegesis* but *enarrationes*, stories. He does not want to explain the psalms without illustrating by them the Christian faith.

The New Testament also shows that we are in good company. When the New Testament authors quote the Old Testament, it is not always to prove that Jesus is the Messiah; rather, it is often to exemplify, clarify, and illuminate the Christian message. They seek and find symbols in the Old Testament by which we see the truth of the faith in a new light. Often it is about the genuine spiritual interpretation, an authentic messianic meaning that belongs to the literal meaning's deeper dimensions. But other times it is simply about playfulness with the text.

The playful, personal reading makes the Scriptures in that way a constantly new and wonderful instrument of the Spirit. The Spirit blows where he wills (Jn 3:8), and if we are following along with his wind in our lives, he will show us unexpected and hidden meanings in the Scriptures and reveal many mysteries about who God is.

4

How the Mystics Interpret the Bible

The most important precept in the Carmelite Rule is to meditate day and night on the law of the Lord and keep watch at prayer. That is why a Carmelite should be deeply familiar with his Bible. All Christian mysticism is nourished by the Bible. But I wish to use examples from the Carmelite mystics since they are the ones that I, as a Carmelite, know best.

The Spiritual Interpretation of the Carmelite Mystics

The first Carmelites found the texts in the First Book of Kings about the prophet Elijah to be a teaching for the whole journey toward the fulfillment of the mystical life. In God's calling to Elijah to hide himself by the brook Cherith (1 Kings 17:2–4), they saw an exhortation to strive for a pure-hearted attitude of life in order to arrive at the experience of God's glory, something that was promised to Elijah when God said: "You shall drink from the brook" (1 Kings 17:4).

This spiritual interpretation, where the Bible texts are read in connection with the deep interior life of prayer and mystical experiences, has ever since blossomed among the great spiritual figures of Carmel.

Saint Teresa of Avila, the reformer of the Carmelite Order, never had a complete Bible at her disposal. At that time, the Bible was not in the vernacular, only in Latin, and, besides that, it was considered unsuitable for a woman uneducated in theology to read it on her own. Nevertheless, she had the Bible as a constant inspiration and touchstone for her spiritual life. She made her own the Bible texts she heard in the liturgy and the rich quotes in spiritual books to which she had access.

There are more than six hundred quotations from Scripture in her writings, often not correctly quoted or with the wrong spelling, since she took them directly from memory and often interpreted them in an extremely personal, playful way. She encourages her sisters, when they do not understand the texts, not to trouble their heads with subtle reflections but, rather, to rejoice in "what a great Lord and God we have. For one word of His will contain within itself a thousand mysteries."[1] And when she does not understand the first words in the Song of Songs, her charming com-

[1] "Meditations on the Song of Songs", chap. 1, in *The Collected Works of St. Teresa of Avila*, trans. Kieran Kavanaugh, O.C.D., and Otilio Rodriguez, O.C.D., vol. 2 (Washington, D.C.: Institute of Carmelite Studies, 1980), pp. 216–17.

mentary is: "I don't understand why this is; and that I don't understand gives me great delight."[2]

Saint Thérèse of Lisieux had access to the whole New Testament and to certain hand-copied parts of the Old Testament. Even her Sisters at the time realized that she had received a special grace to understand and love God's Word in Scripture. One of her first examiners [in the canonization process] wrote: "Is it not wonderful to see how a young girl wanders around with ease in the Scriptures' inspired fields in order to pick out with a sure hand the most diverse texts that best suit her purposes!"

Saint Thérèse had a real hunger for God's Word and did not want to lose a single crumb of it. The Word and the interior prayer that she had two hours a day were for her meeting places that mutually nourished each other. She wrote: "But what, then, is this word? . . . It seems to me that the *word* of Jesus is *Himself*. . . . He, *Jesus*, the *Word*, the *Word* of *God*!"[3]

But Saint John of the Cross (1542–1591) is the one who systematically makes most use of Scripture in order to present the spiritual path and goal for it. In his works, which are comprised of about 900 pages, Scripture is quoted 924 times. Saint John studied the Bible with all of the resources that were offered at the

[2] Ibid., p. 216.
[3] Letter to Celine, July 7, 1894, in *St. Thérèse of Lisieux, General Correspondence*, vol. 2, *1890–1897*, trans. John Clarke, O.C.D. (Washington, D.C.: Institute of Carmelite Studies, 1988), p. 862.

university at that time, and he had an academic foundation. But that does not mean that he felt bound by the literal interpretation. The Bible penetrated his whole life. He heard it daily being read during meals and in the liturgy and had set times for personal reading every day. It seemed obvious for him always to verify his statements with Bible quotes.

He speaks often about the meaning of the text in the spiritual sense, which does not then directly contradict the literal sense. He wants only to reject an all too concrete interpretation. "In this and many other ways souls are misled by understanding God's locutions and revelations according to the letter, according to the outer rind. As has been explained, God's chief objective in conferring these revelations is to express and impart the spirit that is enclosed within the outer rind. This spirit is difficult to understand."[4] "This difficulty in giving a suitable interpretation to God's words reached such a point that even Christ's very disciples, who went about with him, were deceived."[5] To wish to limit God's Word and revelations to what we understand is "like wanting to grasp a handful of air that will escape the hand entirely, leaving only a particle of dust".[6]

---

[4] *The Ascent of Mount Carmel*, II, 19, 5, in *The Collected Works of St. John of the Cross*, trans. Kieran Kavanaugh, O.C.D., and Otilio Rodriguez, O.C.D., 3rd ed. (Washington, D.C.: Institute of Carmelite Studies, 2001), p. 215.

[5] Ibid., 9, p. 217.

[6] Ibid., 10, p. 217.

I want to show in the following how Saint John of the Cross discovers a teaching in the Bible about interior union with God and then how the Bible expressed his mystical experience. His way of reading the Bible has much to teach us, for our reading is often stamped by a one-sided rationalistic way of thinking.

The Bible's Teaching about Union with God

The Bible speaks about God's relationship to his people. Those principles that are valid for this collective relationship can be carried over to the individual relationship between the individual person and God. This transposition of a piece of music to another key is legitimate. God does not act in a capricious way; rather, he acts according to certain principles. Love has its own way of acting. What God does with Israel, he also does with the individual person.

Hosea describes Israel as a faithless wife whom God leads into the desert in order to purify, try her, and show her faithful love. "Therefore, behold, I will allure her, and bring her into the wilderness, and speak tenderly to her" (2:14).

In the same way, man who is seeking God must go out into the desert; he must: "learn silence and quiet the faculties so that God may speak. For in this state, as we pointed out, the natural operations must fade from sight. This is realized when the soul arrives at solitude in these faculties, and God speaks to its heart, as the prophet asserts" (Hos 2:14).[7]

This transposition is all the more justified since everything in the Old Testament points to Christ, he who is the true Israel, who in himself includes everyone who through faith is one with him. And, since everything in the Old Testament points to Christ, it also points to us.

Saint John of the Cross seeks nothing more than God's love in the Bible: he goes directly to the essential. He knows that when God allows man to suffer and endure difficult trials, this also happens because of love. God's wrath is always the wrath of love. According to Saint Augustine, the whole Bible can be summarized in these three words: "God is love" (1 Jn 4:16). He says in a homily: "I must speak to you. Of what else can I speak but of love? If we want to speak about love, we do not need to choose a particular text that gives us an opportunity to preach about love. Wherever we open the Bible, every page speaks about love." When God speaks, it is always to reveal his love. He has nothing else to speak about. He is *only* love.

Like all mystics, Saint John of the Cross discovers a deep dimension in the biblical text that others pass over lightly. When Saint Paul writes: "It is no longer I who live, but Christ who lives in me" (Gal 2:20), this has in principle to do with every Christian, but it is

[7] Ibid., III, 3, 4, p. 274.

completely and fully true only of the one who wholly surrenders himself to God.

"She [the soul] finds in this state a much greater abundance and fullness of God, a more secure and stable peace, and an incomparably more perfect delight than in the spiritual betrothal; here it is as though she were placed in the arms of her Bridegroom. As a result she usually experiences an intimate spiritual embrace, which is a veritable embrace, by means of which she lives the life of God. The words of St. Paul are verified in this soul: *I live, now not I, but Christ lives in me* [Gal 2:20]."[8]

When Saint John of the Cross reads the Psalm verse "Fortitudinem meam ad te custodiam" (I will keep my strength to thee, Psalm 58:10, Vulgate), he sees in these words an exact expression of the total union that man experiences with God. Man says: "My every act is love." He gives this commentary: "All the ability of my soul and body (memory, intellect, and will, interior and exterior senses, appetites of the sensory and spiritual parts) move in love and because of love. Everything I do I do with love, and everything I suffer I suffer with the delight of love."[9]

"He has lifted up the lowly", as it says in Mary's hymn of praise, the Magnificat; "he has filled the hungry with good things" (see Lk 1:52–53). We think perhaps of materially needy people, but for Saint John of the Cross, these words have to do with the person who

[8] *The Spiritual Canticle*, 22, 5, in *Collected Works*, p. 562.
[9] Ibid., 28, 8, p. 586.

has renounced all desires, become completely empty
of all selfish desires, and therefore is filled with God's
peace: "Hence this divine onslaught caused by God in
the soul, like resounding rivers, fills everything with
peace and glory. . . . The divine water filling the low
places of her humility and the voids of her appetites."[10]

By digging deeper into the deep dimensions of the
words, we do not deviate from the literal meaning;
quite the contrary, it is just in this way that we expose
it. If with the literal meaning we mean only what the
human author chose to express, it is clear that we must
often go beyond it. For Saint John of the Cross, the
Bible is first and foremost the Word of God, and the
only important thing for him is to understand what
God has intended. Often the inspired author does not
understand himself what he has written. He understands and interprets the words on a certain level, but
God, who makes use of him, understands them on
another plane. That is why the spiritual interpretation
many times is the only right one. To wish stubbornly
to hold fast to what the author consciously chose to
express often means to miss the actual message.

In a masterly, authoritative chapter in the *Ascent of
Mount Carmel*, which we would wish to recommend to
all fundamentalists, Saint John of the Cross shows how
we can totally misunderstand God when we interpret
the texts of the Bible according to their direct, literal
wording. "God is immense and profound, he usually

[10] Ibid., 14, 9, p. 528.

includes in his prophecies, locutions, and revelations other ways, concepts, and ideas remarkably different from the meaning we generally find in them."[11] He warns not to take God's Word literally and see only the surface. Too great a fidelity to the literal meaning can block the way to the actual meaning of the text.

"By his words, God always refers to the more important and profitable meaning," writes Saint John, "whereas humans will refer the words to a less important sense, in their own way and for their own purpose, and thus be deceived. . . . We see this in David's messianic prophecy. . . . (You shall rule all nations with an iron rod, and dash them to pieces like a vessel of clay). [Ps 2:9]."[12]

"Truly, truly, I say to you, he who believes in me will also do the works that I do; and greater works than these" (Jn 14:12). In certain circles, this text is quoted gladly and often, and it is thought that it shows that there are no limits to the miracles that can be done if one only believes in Jesus. But it is forgotten that the very greatest works happen in the sacraments. When a single person becomes transformed at Baptism into a child of God, there is a greater miracle than when Lazarus was raised to life.

Here we see how important it is to read the Bible in the Church and within the whole Christian tradition's perspective. No one has received so much of the Holy Spirit that he can be sure to be able to understand,

[11] *Ascent of Mount Carmel* II, 19, 1, p. 213.
[12] Ibid., 12, p. 218.

completely alone by himself, what God has revealed in his Word.

Besides, it is not the New Testament that has founded the Church but, rather, the New Testament has come into being in the Church, and it is the Church that decided which texts would have divine authority.

How Saint John of the Cross discovers a teaching in the Bible about the soul's union with God can be illustrated by a typical example. God reveals himself in the Old Testament in the cloud. "As often as God communicated . . . he appeared in darkness."[13] Saint John refers to Moses, Job, the Psalms, etc. The cloud means that God is inaccessible, and we cannot see his essence in this life. The Old and New Testaments are in agreement about this.

As proof, Saint John quotes three texts that to a certain degree form a trilogy. (1) God answers Moses when he prays to see God's glory: "you cannot see my face; for man shall not see me and live" (Ex 33:20). Moses is allowed to see God from the back (v. 23). (2) "No one has ever seen God" (Jn 1:18). (3) "What no eye has seen, nor ear heard, nor the heart of man conceived, what God has prepared for those who love him" (1 Cor 2:9).[14]

The cloud expresses God's incomprehensibility, his inaccessibility. But at the same time, it is nevertheless true that the cloud transmits contact with God. It is *in* the cloud that we meet God. The cloud symbol-

[13] Ibid., 9, 3, p. 177.
[14] Ibid., 8, 4, p. 175.

izes, therefore, the faith that in this life is our only means to having direct contact with God. "All of this darkness signifies the obscurity of faith with which the divinity is clothed while communicating itself to the soul."[15] For God communicates himself. By faith we truly know him, but in a hidden way. In the cloud is the darkness of faith. God is at the same time the one who withdraws and the one who gives himself, incomprehensible and completely present. He *shows himself* as *invisible:* he is present and absent.

The Bible Expresses the Mystical Experience of Saint John of the Cross

When Saint John of the Cross tries to describe the highest mystical experience, he incessantly stumbles up against the limitation of human language. In this situation, he takes his refuge in the Bible, which does also consist of human words but, at the same time, is inspired and, as such, is a divine language. The language of the Bible is a translation of the divine chosen by God himself. This language is charged with divine thoughts and, therefore, comes closest to the mystery of God. It allows us more than merely human language so that we may realize something of what a person can experience when God works in him.

The Bible is, besides this, an objective language that is known by all Christians. It is a particularly special

[15] Ibid., 9, 3, p. 177.

joy when in the writing of the mystics we come across a Bible text that we have read often but whose content expresses possibilities we have never discovered. When a mystic with the help of such a text expresses his deep interior experience, the text opens itself for the one who reads the interpretation. He reads with the joy both of recognition (he has read this text many times before) and of surprise that there is a great chance that the text at a later reading will again reveal more of its deep content. So we learn little by little to read the Bible in depth; to discover the deep dimensions in it.

"O Jesus!" cries Saint Teresa of Avila when she describes the definitive union with God, "Who would know the many things there must be in Scripture to explain this peace of soul!"[16]

Saint John of the Cross points out often that it is completely impossible to relate what the person experiences when she is visited by God. When he speaks about the "many afflictions" that the soul undergoes in the night of the spirit, he writes: "Doubtless, all that we can possibly say would fall short of expressing what this night really is. Through the texts already quoted [from Scripture] we have some idea of it."[17]

Job, Lamentations, and the Psalms are the three books that best express the mystic's dark side.

To describe the light side of the mystic, he turns

---

[16] *Interior Castle*, 7, 3, 13, in *Collected Works of St. Teresa of Avila*, 2:443.
[17] *The Dark Night of the Soul*, II, 7, 2, in *Collected Works of St. John of the Cross*, p. 406.

particularly to the Song of Songs. He loves the Song of Songs more than any other book in the Bible. On his death bed, he wanted the Song of Songs to be read to him. "What precious pearls", he whispered. His *Spiritual Canticle* was inspired by the Song of Songs. We could almost call it an original and free poetic writing of it.

Is it not strange that the most profane of all the books of the Bible (it is so profane and sensual that we sometimes wonder if it did not become a part of the Bible by mistake) is most suitable to relate the very highest mystical experiences? No, perhaps it is not so unusual. The Song of Songs sings about the only thing that is important in this life, about the only thing for which we were created, about love. And it does it with passion and enthusiasm. There is in it an irresistible faith in love. "Many waters cannot quench love, neither can floods drown it. If a man offered for love all the wealth of his house, it would be utterly scorned" (8:7).

This extraordinary lyric shows how the world could have been if we had not lost paradise. Love is enough in itself. Here we are not speaking about God. Nor about innocence or sin. Here we find ourselves on a level that is beyond these categories. Here we are in paradise. This is how God intended love, so absolute, so sovereign.

This love alludes to the new fire that the New Adam came to enkindle on the earth (Lk 12:49). It points to the wedding dance in heaven, to love between Christ

and the Church, between Christ and every Christian.
Such is the Christian life. It is such that it ought to be.
These two who love each other, who enjoy each other
"among the lilies", are the great Lover and his bride,
the soul. It is a pity, says Hans Urs von Balthasar, that
the erotic element of the Song of Songs has been lost
in theology, resulting in "a desiccation of theology".[18]
And it can only be repaired by being steeped once again
in the very heart of the "love mystery" of Scripture.
In contrast to the Jewish Talmud commentary, most
Christian exegetes are in agreement in their opinion
that the author of the Song of Songs thought merely
of human love. "No poet who intended to express
something else—namely, Yhwh's love for his people
—would have written in so totally profane and areli-
gious a fashion and with such wholehearted abandon
to the joys of the senses."[19] But this love is in itself
prophecy; it does not need to be said. The allegory is
not something that is added on afterward. This love is
allegory. "Ubi caritas et amor, Deus ibi est" (Where
there is charity and love, God is there). All love points
to God, in particular the exclusive and faithful love
that is described here.

It is not strange that Saint John of the Cross quotes

---

[18] *Explorations in Theology*, vol. 1, *The Word Made Flesh*, trans.
A.V. Littledale with Alexander Dru (San Francisco: Ignatius Press,
1989), pp. 124–25.

[19] Hans Urs von Balthasar, *The Glory of the Lord*, vol. 6, *Theology: The Old Covenant*, trans. Brian McNeil, C.R.V., and Erasmo
Leiva-Merikakis (San Francisco: Ignatius Press, 1991), p. 133.

the Song of Songs untiringly. The Christian life has for him nothing to do with objectivity and cold duty; it is an adventure of love.

> The second step causes a person to search for God unceasingly. When the bride said that seeking him by night in her bed (when in accord with the first step of love she was languishing), she did not find him, she added: *I will rise up and seek him whom my soul loves* (Song 3:1–3), which as we said the soul does unceasingly. . . . The soul goes about so solicitously on this step that it looks for its Beloved in all things. In all its thoughts it turns immediately to the Beloved; in all converse and business it at once speaks about the Beloved; when eating, sleeping, keeping vigil, or doing anything else, it centers all its care on the Beloved, as we pointed out in speaking of the anxious longings of love.[20]

The allegory lies in the very nature of the thing. To see human love as revelation, reflection, traces of the divine, does not diminish it. On the contrary, it is only then that we truly discover its value. That is why Saint John does not deviate from the text's literal meaning when he sees and uses it as an expression for the soul's love for God. The spiritual sense lies in the very literal one, not outside of it.

There are also obviously occasions when Saint John of the Cross reads a spiritual content into it precisely in order to seek it there. When he speaks of faith in the *Spiritual Canticle*, he thinks of the Psalm verse: "The

[20] *Dark Night of the Soul*, II, 19, 2, p. 88.

wings of a dove covered with silver, its pinions with green gold" (68:13). The dove represents faith for him. The dove's wings, that is, the truths of the faith, are silver plated, but under this silver there is the gold, God himself.

"Faith, consequently, gives and communicates God himself to us, but covered with the silver of faith. Yet it does not for this reason fail to give him to us truly. Were someone to give us a gold vase plated with silver we would not fail to receive a gold vase merely because of it being silver plated."[21]

This is a playful interpretation. David had surely not thought of faith when he described the dove, but as has already been pointed out, the words of Scripture, because they are God's Word, have unlimited possibilities. A person can receive a certain light so that he, in a particular text, discovers a hidden meaning that God places there for him personally, without it being directly in the literal meaning's extension. In this way, every Christian who lets himself be filled with this Spirit finds a personal and substantial nourishment in Scripture. Such an interpretation is not universally applicable and shall therefore not be used as a proof or be considered true exegesis. God gives this meaning to a certain person but not to the whole Church.

That a scriptural text can have many meanings is something that almost all mystics have taken for granted, at least in practice. Saint Bernard of Clairvaux writes that

---

[21] *Spiritual Canticle*, 12, 4, p. 517.

since the Spirit has spoken to man once, each one may seek the nourishment he needs. Here there is a certain amount of freedom. But a freedom that presupposes prayer. It is the Spirit who shall show the way so that we find just the food of which we are in need.

God, who is living and present in his Word, meets every person in his own personal conditions and circumstances. The Scriptures have a completely personal message to each person, while at the same time they embrace and direct the whole human family.

For the one who is open and sensitive, there is hardly any risk that Bible reading will be boring.

5

Praying with the Psalms

"The word is very near you; it is in your mouth."
(Deuteronomy 30:14)

God speaks to us in the Bible, especially in the Psalms. God gives us the words with which we answer. God's Word places the words in our mouths. Why should we create poor words ourselves when God makes it so easy for us and gives us his own words?

To Pray with God's Own Words

It is easy to have a taste for the Psalms when we are aware that it is God himself who has given us these prayers. Everything that God does and gives has an openness, a breadth, and a width that make it possible for each one to feel at home, and the mystics show how the Psalms are interpreted in many ways.

One of the mysteries of the Psalms' openness and multiple meanings is that here, as in the whole Bible, God speaks in images. What is typical of images is that they unite two apparently incompatible characteristics;

they are, namely, both concrete and open. An abstract understanding always remains abstract and therefore gives an impression of unreality. Reality is always concrete. To say that God is good and merciful is not always effective, but the parable of the prodigal son leaves hardly anyone unmoved.

That images and symbols, besides being concrete, are also open, we all know. A picture points in a direction but does not mark any borders. That Jesus is the Lamb of God or the Lion of Judah can be interpreted in many ways that can be thought to contradict each other but that fundamentally, nevertheless, do not do that.

There is also a mystery that explains the feeling of freedom and boundlessness we get when we read the Psalms. The prayers of the Psalms are inserted into a history, Israel's history, which makes everything that is said connected with the past and future. Everything points backward and forward. Backward, perhaps as far as the beginning of man. When I pray Psalm 139: "My frame was not hidden from you, when I was being made in secret" (v. 15), my thoughts go out spontaneously to the first man that God formed from the earth. When I pray: "For the enemy has pursued me; he has crushed my life to the ground" (Ps 143:3), it is not about an abstract enemy. Everything I have read and know about the persecution of Israel by its enemies, especially the Egyptians, is brought to life and is included in the meaning of the word "enemy".

But many words point forward to Christ and his

kingdom. When I read: "The LORD builds up Jerusalem; he gathers the outcasts of Israel" (Ps 147:2), I cannot help thinking of the heavenly Jerusalem that the Lord is building up and of all mankind, whom I hope he will gather there.

We understand Saint Augustine when he says: "Psalterium meum, gaudium meum" (My psalter is my joy). No other prayer book can be compared to the one that God himself has authored for us.

We Pray with the Same Words as Jesus

During his life on earth, Jesus prayed the Psalms. The same can be said of the Virgin Mary. "We are right in believing", says the General Instruction of the Liturgy of the Hours, "that [Jesus] took part in public prayers, in the synagogues, which he entered on the Sabbath 'as his custom was' (Luke 4:16), and in the temple, which he called a house of prayer (Matthew 21:13), as well as in the private prayers which devout Israelites would recite regularly every day. He used the traditional blessing of God at meals. This is expressly mentioned in connection with the multiplication of the loaves, the Last Supper, the meal at Emmaus."[1]

Jesus commanded us to do what he himself did. He said often that we should pray *in his name*. We truly pray in his name when we use the same words he did.

---

[1] General Instruction of the Liturgy of the Hours, no. 4, in *The Liturgy of the Hours according to the Roman Rite* (Libreria Editrice Vaticana; Washington, D.C.: USCCB, 2011), 1:23.

It is something great to know that the psalms I now pray were prayed and sung by Jesus, that he made them his own prayer, as an expression of his own feelings, his love for the Father, his trust, his joy, but also his anguish, his indignation, his protest against injustice.

It does not sound at all pharisaical to pray: "Vindicate me, O LORD, for I have walked in my integrity" (Ps 26:1), when we know that it is Jesus who prays in that way. And then we may even pray that way, for we are in him, *filii in Filio* (sons in the Son), and we pray in his name.

But can Jesus have prayed a psalm that is a confession of sin? Can he have said: "Have mercy on me, O God, according to your merciful love; according to your abundant mercy blot out my transgressions" (51:1–2)? Of course! Such a psalm is more suitable in his mouth than in ours. He has taken all the sins of mankind upon himself, "For our sake he made him to be sin who knew no sin, so that in him we might become the righteousness of God" (2 Cor 5:21).

When we pray the psalms, it is always an agreement with this prayer. Sometimes it is easy to recognize Jesus' prayer, to hear him sing or sigh. Can we do anything but think of him when we pray: "They stare and gloat over me; they divide my garments among them, and for my clothing they cast lots" (Ps 22:17–18)? Or also: "I shall not die, but I shall live, and recount the deeds of the LORD" (Ps 118:17). In some way the whole Psalter is about death and life, and no one has lived through the passing over from death to life so consciously and dramatically as Jesus. It is the Paschal Mystery, his *pascha*, that is to say, the Passover from death to life, which is central in the mystery of Christ.

The Vengeance Psalms

It is surely more difficult to recognize Jesus' prayers in the so-called vengeance psalms. How can he who praised the meek as blessed take such words in his mouth? But Jesus is not only a meek Lamb of God. He is also the one who hurls curses in the face of the Pharisees.

When we read his sevenfold: "Woe to you, scribes and Pharisees, hypocrites", in Matthew 23, we understand that he did not need to skip over certain vengeance psalms that are offensive to our ears. He was also faithful to these! Is there such a great difference between the curses in the Psalms and his word to the Pharisees: "You serpents, you brood of vipers, how are you to escape being sentenced to hell?" (Mt 23:33)? Nor is Saint John particularly gentle toward the "many antichrists" who "went out from us, but they were not of us" (1 Jn 2:18, 19).

When Jesus accuses the Pharisees, and when he prays the vengeance psalms, it is not for him a way to give vent to his aggression. For us, it is perhaps that, and it can be beneficial to be able to give vent to one's repressed feelings to God in the form of prayer. Jesus

saw deeper. Enemies for him were never personal enemies, but enemies of God's people and, thus, God's
enemies. They were people who sought to prevent
God from realizing his plan of salvation. Not to react
to such enemies would be cruel toward mankind. For
Jesus, it is a question of clearing away all hindrances
so that God's love can freely flow over mankind.

But Jesus sees, he looks deeper. He sees that these
enemies are puppets in the power of Satan and that
there is a cosmic battle going on between light and
darkness. "For we are not contending against flesh and
blood, but against the principalities, against the powers, against the world rulers of this present darkness,
against the spiritual hosts of wickedness in the heavenly places" (Eph 6:12).

Nor is it persons that Jesus wants to remove but,
rather, the behavior of some persons. When he con-
demns the actions of the godless, he is at the same time
seeking their hearts. And it is permitted to hope that
he also finally finds them and that they accept him.

The prayer book of Israel undergoes an inner transformation when Jesus makes it his own prayer book.
We can no longer object that the Psalms belong to the
Old Testament and that we live in the New Testament.
The Psalter now receives a New Testament stamp. By
the fact that Christ prays it, its content becomes chris-
tified when we pray it; we hear Christ pray, and we
discover the same deep dimension in the text as he did.

God knew from the beginning the prayers of the

Psalter would receive their full meaning, which they
bore latently, only when the Word became flesh and
pronounced them himself.

If we have learned to recognize Christ's prayer, the
reading of the Psalter becomes an occasion of constantly new discoveries. We are never finished with it.

A Song of Praise to Our God

The Psalter is an invaluable gift to Israel and to the
Church. And the very finest, the very greatest aspect
of this gift is that it teaches us to praise God. "It is
good to give thanks to the LORD, to sing praises to
your name, O Most High" (Ps 92:1).

Man is most himself and realizes his greatest po-
tential when he praises and thanks God. Then he is
happy, then he enters into "the joy of the Lord", then
he is precisely as he is intended by God to be: completely free of self and directed toward him. Nothing
is so healing as to praise God. In and with the song
of praise, man's original direction returns; the verti-
cal direction. When he praises God, and thus leaves
himself, he comes home to himself. He is created as
relationship with God, as *ecstatic*, as taken out of himself.

When man praises God for his own sake, *propter mag-
nam gloriam tuam* (for your great glory), he regains his
condition in paradise and becomes completely what he
actually is. "I will sing to the LORD as long as I live;
I will sing praise to my God while I have being" (Ps

104:33–34). When we please God by praising him, we also become happy ourselves. When we rejoice over God, we participate in Jesus' rejoicing in his Father. This rejoicing is his fundamental attitude.

"In that same hour he rejoiced in the Holy Spirit and said, 'I thank you, Father, Lord of heaven and earth'" (Lk 10:21).

By constantly letting go of ourselves anew in praise and being taken up in God, we are also continually born anew. We live in the joy of the resurrection. Then we can also bear much. We can truly not blame the Psalmist for repressing or fleeing the hard reality. There is hardly any prayer in the history of mankind where one so unrestrainedly gives expression to his pain, his despair, his revolt.

In the Psalter, we always find ourselves on two levels at the same time. The level of evil, with its human and cosmic catastrophes—and God's level, where his omnipotence and mercy triumph over all. On the one level, everything only becomes worse, and we are on the way to the final destruction. On the other level, everything is on the way to becoming well, yes, everything in some way already is well. As an illustration of this, a quote from a person who lives very close to God is fitting here.

Even if I find myself in human pain or in the midst of my own misery and weakness, his glory is nevertheless at the same time so dazzlingly apparent, as though in another dimension. Certainly the perishable, the visible, the sometimes very painful reality is the invisible glory that continuously pulses forth in the eternity that is right in our midst. Here the judgment has already passed. What cannot last in eternity has already lost its existence. Sin has no *actual* reality. Sin is only that man blinds himself to the truth. But however much he wishes to blind himself, the truth and the true reality are still what they are.

The process of sanctification, life in the spirit of the Beatitudes, is little by little to have one's eyes opened, until they can finally see that *all is good* if only our eyes are open. To comfort is no longer a virtue because there can no longer be anything but comfort. The whole world rests in a cradle of security and tenderness, and nothing can separate it from the love of God in Christ Jesus. Through him, with him, in him, everything is glory without end.

In the Psalter, there are both levels. We could call them the *provisional* plane of reality and the *final* plane of reality. On the one plane, we see the periphery; on the other, the deep dimension: on the one plane, we use our human eyes; on the other, we borrow God's eyes. But these two planes are not equal. The lamentation psalms usually end up flowing out into comfort; the initial revolt eventually melts away and is replaced by surrender. The complaint is a way to greater trust.

Even Israel knows that the actual reality is good, that everything rests in God's hand and is therefore fundamentally good; it is clear from the very name these poetic songs have received. In Hebrew, they are called *tehillim*, which means to sing hymns of praise;

in Greek, *psalmoi*, songs that are sung with accompaniment. Even if there are quite a few complaints and sighs, the same texts are nevertheless called hymns of praise. In the midst of all darkness, we praise God because he is Light and because "the light shines in the darkness" (Jn 1:5).

Many of the people of our time recognize themselves best in the lamentation psalms. They find most comfort in expressing their sorrow and desperation before God. To give vent to their pent-up feelings does them good and gives them consolation. And that is excellent. Jesus himself said: "Come to me, all who labor and are heavy laden, and I will give you rest" (Mt 11:28). But if religion serves *only* to comfort us in our need, there is a risk of it doing us a disservice. Then we are never freed from our little, narrow world. Then religion can easily become a sedative that relieves our pains, a kind of opium; just what in our time people so often blame religion for being.

We see in the Gospel that Jesus untiringly heals the sick but that at the same time he also wants to make everyone his disciples, people who willingly take up their cross and follow him unto death. He wants to free us from ourselves. He himself gives his life for us, but he wants us to have a share in his own joy, which is a joy of giving. It consists of his blessedness, which he has in communion with his Father. He speaks from experience when he says, "It is more blessed to give than to receive" (Acts 20:35).

It is just this that we learn in the Psalms. We are

permitted to complain and sigh sometimes; we need to express ourselves. But the Psalter is not a collection of hymns of lamentation. The emphasis lies on praise. When we praise and bless God, we *give* ourselves and are also allowed to experience that it *is* more blessed to give than to receive. There is a wonderful amount of complaint and praise in the Psalms with a marked predominance of praise. We are created, not to complain, but to praise.

That God has created us in this way does not depend on the fact that he needs our praise in order to be happy. There is truly no lack of praise in the Holy Trinity, where the Father empties himself in the glorification of the Son and the Son in glorifying the Father. It is for our sake that God has created us for praise. A text from the Catholic liturgy expresses it in a perfect way: "For, although you have no need of our praise, yet our thanksgiving is itself your gift, since our praises add nothing to your greatness but profit us for salvation, through Christ our Lord."[2]

If we do not feel at home in the world of the Psalms, if we would rather not pray with the Psalms, we ought to ask ourselves whether we are actually interested in God. For if we do not gladly and willingly praise God, it is probably because we have not understood who God is. If we begin to realize something of God's holiness and greatness, of the *great things* he has done for us, we must overflow with joy and thanksgiving. Then

[2] Common Preface IV, in *The Roman Missal*, 3rd ed. (Libreria Editrice Vaticana; Washington, D.C.: USCCB, 2011), p. 616.

we become like those Icelandic geysers that suddenly erupt and spew out hot water. Then we are grateful that here are hymns of praise written by a people who knew what jubilation is (Ps 89:16); praise, by which we may give expression to our admiration and that helps us not to forget how much good he has done (Ps 103:2).

The praises of Israel are at the same time *remembrance*: we praise God for nature; that he created man so great, but above all for the great deeds he has done for his people. What applies to the whole Bible, that it is the good memory of mankind, is especially true of the Psalms. It refreshes our memory and in that way gives us fuel for our praise.

"Man is the only creature that is a prisoner of his past", writes the French philosopher Paul Ricoeur (b. 1913). It can seem like that, and on a certain level it is true. We all carry with us some wounds that are the consequences of what we have experienced or done. But on another level, it is not at all true. Instead of imprisoning us, the memory can also free us. Alongside of the narcissistic memory that causes us to lick our wounds, there is also an Easter memory, a Resurrection memory that directs us to God's good deeds and causes us in a certain way to share in God's own memory; he remembers his covenant. This Resurrection memory frees us from our evil past. It is even possible to discover God's *visitation* in the difficult thing that afflicted us.

This good memory makes us Eucharistic people,

that is to say, people who are filled with gratitude and praise. We received this Resurrection memory at our Baptism, but most of us make use of it all too seldom. We are so forgetful. We are like Israel, which was constantly tempted to forget God's great deeds and which needed prophets to remind it again and again of everything God had done. "O my people, remember" (Mic 6:5).

The Psalms are such prophets, refreshing our memory and helping us to shake off our forgetfulness; then the sources of praise are freed and are themselves that hymn of praise. Every time we pray a psalm of praise or thanksgiving, we exchange our narcissistic memory for our Easter memory.

In the Liturgy of the Hours, the Church has arranged it so that even those psalms that are actually more lamentation than praise nevertheless receive a character of praise. "Glory be to the Father and to the Son and to the Holy Spirit." We can thank Saint Benedict for that. It was he who decided that every psalm should end with the praise: "Glory be to the Father . . .", while everyone rises and reverently bows in honor of the Trinity.

Thy Heart Shall Wonder and Be Enlarged (Isaiah 60:5, Douay-Rheims)

The prayer we create ourselves is often rather narrow, simply because our heart is narrow. Our narrow heart must open, widen. "Our heart is wide", writes Saint

Paul to the Corinthians, "You are not restricted by us, but you are restricted in your own affections. In return—I speak as to children—widen your hearts also" (2 Cor 6:11–13). The Psalter is a key that opens our heart. It leads us into boundlessness both in time and space.

When we pray the Psalter, we are not left to our subjective feelings. We enter into an objective prayer that is given to us. This can seem unmodern; not at all suitable to the modern-day person's needs. We want to be spontaneous in our prayer, honest before God. To read prayers that others have prepared seems artificial. Jesus, however, was not afraid that our prayer would be artificial when he himself prepared a prayer for us; namely, the Our Father. He knew that in the area of prayer, we are children. As a child needs to hear his parents and teachers speak and must be instructed in grammar in order to express himself understandably and correctly, so there is also a grammar of prayer that we have learned with the help of prayers that have been formulated beforehand.

If we are completely left to ourselves, our prayer remains extremely poor, self-centered, and fundamentally dishonest. It is absurd to believe that we are honest when we express everything that is in our heads. Man is more than the thoughts and feelings he experiences at the moment. Freud's free association does not give a just picture of man. There are deeper levels in him, and in order to discover them he needs the help of others.

As the small pray-ers that we are, we need the help

of great pray-ers so that the prayer will gradually rise up out of the very deepest part of ourselves.

Fundamentally, there is no real contradiction between subjective and objective, presupposing that we take the word subjective or subjectively in all its meaning. The objective prayer that I find in the Psalter helps me to discover myself, my subjectivity, that which constitutes me as subject, namely, my relationship to God and to mankind.

There is more in me than what I say when I spontaneously express myself before God. An objective prayer can give me access to that more. It does not alienate me, make me foreign to myself; rather, it personalizes me. It unlocks my subjectivity. What I pray about, everything I express when I pray the Psalms, was actually within me, but I did not know it.

When I read or sing the Psalm verses, I recognize the content as my own, and then I am also able to experience that my spirit is much wider, more spacious than I thought. I have a heart that contains the whole universe.

To pray with the words of the Psalter demands a certain humility. We pray with words that are not immediately our own. We recognize our dependency on others. We do that which Jesus did throughout his life: We say, "Amen. Yes, Father"; we confirm that word which the Father speaks; we entrust ourselves to the word that is given. We refrain from praying with our own words in order, instead, to pray with words we have received and give to God "of his own gifts". We

open our heart and wait for what is coming; that which
God himself places in the pray-er's mouth.

A Universal Prayer

The Psalter is Christ's prayer; it is he who is the *I* of the
Psalter. Christ is the universal man. He has identified
himself with every man. He has taken everything human upon himself. He represents, not only the beautiful, pious, virtuous people, but even the outcasts,
psychologically sick, despairing, sinful people. It is he
who leads their plea in the Psalter.

Why should those feelings that the Psalms express
need to be in harmony with my feelings just now?
Am I so self-absorbed that I cannot open myself to
others' feelings, to that which lives in my fellowmen
and therefore also in Christ? Shall I not do as he did
and open myself to my brother and my sister and carry
their pleading in my prayer? That very discrepancy I
experience between the psalm and my own frame of
mind is a challenge that invites me to go out of my
own narrow house and enter into what others think
and experience.

In that way, I discover one of prayer's deepest dimensions; that it also has a set representative, vicari-
ous character. As long as I do not leave my ivory tower
attitude, my prayer is not truly Christian. I am called
to place myself at the disposal of all who are not able
to express their sorrows and their anguish, their revolt
and their despair before God. The prayer of the Psalter

gives me an opportunity to allow all of that into my
heart and to transform it there into prayer. I learn to
rejoice with those who rejoice, to cry with those who
cry (Rom 12:15). I learn to carry others' burdens and
so fulfill the law of Christ, which is love (Gal 5:14). I
lend my tongue and my mouth to others who become
mute as soon as they stand before God.

Thanks to this prayer, no one stands outside of the
world of prayer any longer. All are taken in, everyone
is included. Such a prayer becomes truly Catholic, that
is to say, all-embracing, universal.

Instead of praying: "God have mercy on all who suffer", I pray Psalm 6: "O LORD, rebuke me not in your
anger, nor chasten me in your wrath. Have mercy on
me, O LORD, for I am languishing; O LORD, heal me,
for my bones are troubled" (Ps 6:1–2). I say *I* and *me*,
and a superficial listener could think that I was thinking only of myself. But this *I* is not my private *I* but
the *I* of suffering mankind; that of the One to whom
Pilate pointed when he said: "Behold the Man." Just
for that reason, that I want to be one with him, Christ,
and with all those he represents, can I say *I* without
my prayer being a self-centered prayer.

When we allow the *I* in the Psalms to expand to a
universal *I* of mankind, we also become less shocked
at the vengeance psalms when we learn to place ourselves in the situations of others; also in the situations
of those who are tortured and degraded in their human dignity. And when we then bring their plea before God, it is not so unusual that we protest violently!

There is in every person a sound sense of justice and the insight that the evil that has destroyed the order must be punished so that the order can be restored. The teaching about purgatory and hell is the Christian confirmation of this innate insight and shows that the protest against injustice and oppression are within God himself.

If I prayed for vengeance, for the violence and injustice to which I was personally subjected, my prayer would perhaps not be completely blameless. Jesus teaches us not to strike back when someone strikes us. But he has not forbidden us to defend our fellowmen who are being treated violently; on the contrary, he wants us to be ready to lay down our lives for them. Since the *I* in the Book of Psalms is not simply my personal *I* but, rather, that of mankind, my prayer about revenge is fundamentally a work of love: I protest against the evil to which my brother and sister are subjected and want justice.

There is no feeling that does not have its expression in the Psalms. For that very reason, the Psalter is such a durable, lasting prayer book. We never tire of it. The endless variation of thoughts and feelings we meet there makes it possible for us to pray it without limits. After two thousand years, the Church has not had enough.

The universal dimension of the Psalter also makes it an ecumenical prayer book. No person can remain unmoved by it. It is, as a matter of fact, used in all Christian denominations, and Christianity has it in common with Israel. Nothing points so clearly and so concretely to our Old Testament roots and our connection with our older brothers and sisters from Israel as precisely this, that we pray to God with the same words.

All Christians, together with the Jewish people, form one great choir, whose common song is itself a prayer of unity, whether we are conscious of it or not.

6

On Reading the Bible Regularly

"Let the word of Christ dwell in you richly."
(Colossians 3:16)

Different Ways of Reading the Bible

There are many different ways of reading the Bible. Everyone must find his own way, that which corresponds with his personal development. We do not read the Bible the same way throughout our lives. As our relationship to God deepens and intensifies, the meeting with his Word also changes us. We listen to a friend differently from the way we listen to a stranger.

It is, for example, meaningful to read the Bible with the thought of its historical development. Since God's revelation is a historic process and salvation history, it is important to have some insight into that historical development and to see how God's plan of salvation is eventually realized and grows toward "the day of Christ" (Phil 1:10), the coming of Christ in the world.

The Bible can also be read from cover to cover, *lectio continua*, while one reads a good commentary to the text along with it.

We can underline texts that throw light on a certain theme, for example, longing, joy, peace. Anyone who reads the Bible with his search directed toward a certain object can make unexpected discoveries. An additional advantage of this method is that our eyes immediately fall on the underlined text when we open our Bible later. In this way, the grace we receive is actualized when we understand our underlined text and read it once again.

With the help of a concordance or a Bible dictionary, it is easy to do theme studies and look up all the texts that have to do with a certain subject. What does the Bible say about conversion, trust, poverty, the Holy Spirit? It is obvious that the one way of reading the Bible does not exclude the other. At the same time as we perhaps read through the whole Bible successively, we can every evening (or every morning) have a short meditative reading from the beginning in order to read the Bible as God's message to us personally. I should not content myself with merely historical, objective reading. Bible reading is always meant to be something of a *lectio divina*, divine reading.

"Lectio Divina"

"Holy Scripture", says *Dei Verbum*, "must be read and interpreted in the sacred spirit in which it was written.''[1] That is why Scripture reading is called *lectio divina*, divine reading, not only because it is God's Word that one reads, but also because God is with the one who reads. We are always two who are reading: the Holy Spirit and I.

Lectio divina is as old as Christianity and actually older. The Jewish rabbis had already said that God's law was his presence to which we open ourselves by reading, meditation, and prayer. Christianity has inherited this way of reading the Scriptures from Judaism. ''But as for you,'' writes Saint Paul to Timothy ''continue in what you have learned and . . . knowing . . . how from childhood you have been acquainted with the Sacred Writings'' (2 Tim 3:14–15). The Church Fathers read the Scriptures in this way, and during the Middle Ages one spoke explicitly and systematically about three (moments) that make up *lectio divina*, namely, *lectio* (reading), *meditatio* (meditation), and *oratio* (prayer).

During the late Middle Ages, this form of Scripture reading began to degenerate. Instead of letting it flow out into prayer, they sought arguments that could be used in theological debate. In the sixteenth century, this form of Bible reading almost disappeared in the Catholic Church with the exception of certain monasteries.[2]

---

[1] *DV* 12.

[2] God's Word, writes John Paul II, is the foremost source of all Christian spirituality. See his Post-synodal Apostolic Exhortation *Vita consecrata* on the Consecrated Life and Its Mission in the Church and in the World (March 25, 1996), no. 94.

The Vatican Council has joined the original tradition and vigorously recommended regular Bible reading: "The sacred synod also earnestly and especially urges all the Christian faithful, especially Religious, to learn by frequent reading of the divine Scriptures. . . . And let them remember that prayer should accompany the reading of Sacred Scripture, so that God and man may talk together."[3]

The Bible is not first of all a book without a seed (Lk 8:11), a seed that contains life. The Bible wants to satisfy our hunger for life. The one who reads it without such a hunger misses the essential part. What is special about the Bible is that the message coincides with the one who conveys the message. God's Word is a Person. To listen to God's Word is to come in contact with Christ, the Word.

The Bible is not a collection of ideas and anecdotes. In it, we meet God, who speaks his Word to us. God's Word has been written down in the Bible so that it can at any time become God's living Word, he who has the words of eternal life (Jn 6:68). There is a way of reading the Bible where God is God, where one reads a text that speaks *about* him. There is another way where God simply is: God speaks directly to me, and I listen and answer. That is *lectio divina*.

An active variation of *lectio divina* that I gladly recommend is what I call meditation in writing. One writes a short meditation, preferably in the form of a

---

[3] *DV* 25.

prayer, about a Bible text, preferably a text from the New Testament. Charles de Foucauld (1858–1916) has filled hundreds of pages with meditations about the Gospels. He installed a little table in front of the altar in the chapel and wrote down his meditations there. There is a risk that the Bible texts no longer speak to us because we have heard and read them so often. When we write, we are forced to go deeper into the text.

If we do not think of anything to write, we can remind ourselves that God's Word consists of promises and challenges. After every sentence, we can ask: What is in this text for me? That is: 1. What does God want of me (exhortation), and 2. What does he promise me? These two, moreover, exhortation and promise, form a unity. It is God's promise that gives us strength to fulfill his will, and his exhortation has no other meaning than to open us to his promise. The Christian life is always both gift and task.

In the old monastic tradition, Scripture reading was intertwined and mixed with interior prayer. The word rumination, chewing, was frequently used. The term comes from Pachomius (ca. 290–346), who founded the first monastic community and wrote a rule for it. One ruminates on the Word, chews it; repeats it again and again. William of Saint Thierry (ca. 1085–1148), a friend of Saint Bernard of Clairvaux, writes in the famous golden epistle to the brothers at Mont Dieu: "In regard to the Scripture, *rumination* differs from ordinary reading just as much as friendship does from a passing acquaintance and as brotherly love does from an occasional greeting. With the daily reading, a mouthful must go down into the stomach of the memory in order to digest it better and so that one can chew it when it comes up again from the stomach."[4] We are encouraged to chew food properly, and we know from experience that food tastes better when we take time to chew it. Coarse bread becomes tastier the longer it is chewed! It is the same with the Word of Scripture; the more we ruminate over it, the more wonderful it tastes. "How sweet are your words to my taste, sweeter than honey to my mouth!" (Ps 119:103). "More to be desired are they than gold, even much fine gold; sweeter also than honey and drippings of honeycomb" (Ps 19:10–11). Thanks to this rumination, we begin to "taste and see that the LORD is good" (Ps 34:8).

We ought always to have a Bible Word to chew on. In some ways, we humans are *ruminators*. We are always chewing on something, often critical thoughts or old disappointments. Would it not be more fruitful to chew on God's Word?

A Concrete Example

1. Reading. Perhaps you read a text from the Gospel of John, for example, between Jesus and the Samaritan woman. "Whoever drinks of the water that I shall give

---

[4] William of Saint Thierry, *The Golden Epistle*, nos. 121–22 (*SC* 223–40; *PL* 184:1).

him will never thirst; the water that I shall give him will become in him a spring of water welling up to eternal life" (4:14).

Let us assume that you remain with the last sentence, the one that emphasizes the image of the spring.

2. Meditation. Meditation was originally, not an intellectual work, but something one did with the mouth. "Os iusti meditabitur sapientiam" is translated as "The mouth of the righteous utters wisdom, and his tongue speaks justice" (Ps 37:30), or even more concretely: *repeat* or *mumble* the word of wisdom. When the Psalmist says "How I love your law! It is my meditation all the day" ("tota die meditatio mea est", 119:97), he does not mean to ponder the law, but to repeat the word of the law unceasingly.

You are doing that now. You repeat the sentence you have chosen many times, while at the same time you personalize it. "The water *you* give shall become a spring in me, welling up to eternal life." If you are alone, you can repeat the word to yourself quietly. By being repeated, the words have the chance to take root in you; they glide from the mouth to the heart.

It is told about Father Matta El Meskeen—he was then still the leader of the Coptic Macarius monastery in Egypt—that a disciple came to him and asked: "Father teach me to pray." Father Matta answered: "Give me your Bible." He opened the New Testament at the beginning of the Letter to the Ephesians, stood upright, lifted his eyes toward heaven, and said: "This is how you should pray."

He read the first verse aloud. After a moment of silence, he repeated slowly every word, two, three times, read the whole verse again, was silent, read the second verse, mumbled it, lifted his arms toward heaven, began to cry . . . and then he continued to read, having completely forgotten that his disciple stood next to him.

3. Prayer. When you have repeated the words a few times and are completely filled by their content, you stop meditating and begin the actual prayer. You can speak lovingly to God or Jesus Christ about what you have meditated on. You can speak of your thirst, of your contrition for having thirsted after bagatelles instead of God. You express your joy and gratitude over the interior spring where waters fill you with eternal life.

Or you can also be still before God in a loving silence. The words have taken root in your heart, and now they can germinate, grow. You do nothing. You only allow it to happen.

When you notice that your thoughts come back and begin to trouble you, you can return to reading. You repeat the whole process. You read until you again find something in which you become absorbed.

Lectio divina is an excellent entryway to interior recollection. At first, and even later, it is usually difficult to remain in God's presence for long periods of time. All possible thoughts rise up to the surface and wander around. Then it can be a great help to read some inspired words of the Bible and thus come away from the disturbing images and memories and return to rest under God's gaze.

Lectio divina in this strict form is naturally not the only way to read the Bible. A whole lifetime would be hardly enough to have time to read through all of the Scriptures. We also need to read the texts more flowingly in order to receive them in their proper context and to be faithful to the whole content. Only in that way are we in a position to explore the depths of *lectio divina*.

The one who wishes to live an intense spiritual life should preferably use many different reading methods alongside each other.

Time and Scripture Reading

It takes time to read the Bible regularly, and time is a commodity that is lacking. At least that is what we think. Man also has a peculiar ability always to find time for non-essential things but not for that which would give him true joy. We leave the most important for last. The intention can be good: when we have cleaned the house and washed the dishes, when everything is in its place and the whole house is in order, *then* we would be able to give ourselves to prayer and reading in peace and quiet. But a house is never completely in order. There are always new things that come up that should and could be done.

We find time for most things. But just that time we had intended to give to Bible reading, just those ten or fifteen minutes, are lacking. There are exactly fifteen minutes too little! Would it help us if the day were a bit longer? Not at all. Once a year, we get an extra hour when in Autumn we change from daylight savings time to normal time—do we find more time for prayer then?

How often does it happen that we suddenly *gain* one or two hours because something we had planned to do was unexpectedly done by another or that invited guests say they cannot come. All of a sudden you have a whole afternoon you did not expect at your disposal. But immediately a great number of important things come up that you would like to do to fill up the free time. Imagine if we had all the time we receive in that way to give to prayer or Scripture reading! Christ's Word would truly live in us in all its richness and with all its wisdom (Col 3:16).

Saint John Chrysostom (ca. 345–407) speaks harsh words to the one who does not realize that Bible reading is so important.

"Some of you perhaps say: I am no monk. But you are mistaken when you believe that the Scriptures only have to do with monks, while you, ordinary believers in the midst of the world, need them much more. There is something that is even more serious and sinful than not reading the Scriptures, namely, to believe that Scripture reading is unnecessary and one does not gain anything from it."[5]

---

[5] *Homilies on Matthew*, II, 10 (*PG* 57:30).

There are moments that are more suitable than others for prayer and Bible reading, especially in the morning and the evening. The morning has the advantage that the Bible reading can *radiate out* over the day and its work. One is equipped to meet the day's many sorts of tasks.

The one who is not too tired in the evening can gladly read the Bible just before going to bed. The evening has a sacred atmosphere. Work no longer troubles one's mind; nature itself goes to rest. The evening's peace promotes the heart's freedom and openness.

It is important that the last thing we do in the evening is something inspiring and valuable. Those thoughts with which we end the day sink down into the unconscious and grow there during the night. During sleep, the unconscious works most actively. That is why it is wise to give it good raw material to work on so that the night bears fruit. One can often notice that the last thought in the evening is the first one in the morning. Why lose our time during sleep when God "gives to his beloved sleep" (Ps 127:2). The unconscious can be filled with God's Word.

How long? I think that ten minutes is the minimum. Five minutes is not enough to enter into the words of Scripture. With prayer and Bible reading, it is the same as with everything that is useful and desirable. It is easier when we do it with a certain regularity. Regularity is a concrete expression of the faithfulness that is an essential element in love. It is something other than iron-hard discipline but also different from sloppiness.

Faithfulness causes one to read not only when it feels good, and it also means that one can make exceptions when there is reason for it. God does not will that we demand the impossible of ourselves, but he is glad when we willingly offer some of our time in order to listen to his Word, even if just at the moment we do not *feel* any particular desire to do it.

There are periods and situations when we do not have the energy or simply do not have the possibility to pray or read. But often we have more energy than we think. It is truly not wrong to create a little more order in our lives. It is extremely fruitful to make a little extra effort to come over the threshold and try to conquer a certain lack of interest or apathy. Love does not consist only in spontaneous motions and actions. It also entails hard work with ourselves.

The one who strives to discipline himself will often fail, it is true. The one who does not try will never fail! And we accuse ourselves of this often and with good reason. But why should we be afraid to fail? There is no progress without many failed attempts. And to the degree that failure causes guilt on our part, there is forgiveness. Our failures create a greater need for forgiveness and can in that way lead us to God. Nor is it so dangerous to reproach oneself as a Christian. Have not all the saints done that? It is an essential part of love to know that one never loves enough, that one always wishes to love more. *One is never totally and completely Christian* even in the best cases; one *becomes* that.

How Is It Done?

One should avoid reading the Bible according to one's own subjective needs. To choose a Bible verse that we believe answers to an actual need is of course not wrong when it happens a few times, but it should not be the general rule. If we choose texts according to our own whims, we reduce the Bible to a book that gives answers to our needs. We look for what we want to find. But the Bible has much more to say to us. It also wants to awaken new questions or give answers to questions we have never thought of. The Bible is in its entirety God's Word. God must have the chance to say to us what he wants to have said.

That is why it is important to have a certain objectivity when we approach God's Word. Only in that way do we show the respect it deserves. What is traditionally called *lectio continua*, continuous reading, guarantees respect. At some time in life, every Christian ought to read the Bible in this way, from cover to cover. But continuous reading is a method that is always suitable for the individual books of the Bible.

For the one who is not yet familiar with the Bible, it is surely best to begin with reading the New Testament from beginning to end.

A more continuous reading of the lectionary first can be followed by a more selective reading. For a more varied reading, we can, for example, take the lectionary for the daily Mass. If one has become more familiar with the Bible, one can in quiet reflection choose the book of the Bible to which one wishes to devote one's time and then go through it in a *lectio continua.*

The one who devotes himself for a longer period of time to the Old Testament can at the same time, for example, keep the contact with the New Testament by a short Gospel reading every evening. In this way, the perspective of the Old Testament is constantly enlightened by the Person of Jesus Christ.

It is also a good idea on Sunday—the Lord's day —to take time for a longer period of Bible reading. One could, for example, read through the whole Bible on Sunday from beginning to end. On weekdays, one could have a more varied program of reading.

To have preferences for certain texts eventually is a normal and healthy development. The more life with God is deepened, the more clearly our personal calling and mission are also formed. Then it is also natural that some Bible texts correspond to this personal path more than others. We gladly return to these texts, we see them continually in a new perspective.

Whenever and however we wish to read, it is most essential that we always and everywhere meet Jesus Christ.

Faith and Openness

Bible reading can bear fruit only for the one who truly believes in the saving power of God's Word. In the whole Bible and above all in the Gospel, we meet Jesus by reading; we come closer to him. In ancient times, there were in the Church two joined containers. In the one was preserved the consecrated bread from Mass; in the other, the book of the Gospel: Jesus' presence under the form of the bread and as the Word of life. In our day, we often see the Bible laid on or before the altar. It is not only homage to a precious book but a profession of faith. We truly believe that the Lord is present in his Word. "He is present in His word", says the Second Vatican Council, "since it is He Himself who speaks when the holy scriptures are read in the Church."[6] To read the Bible is constantly to gather strength from the source of life. "For in the sacred books, the Father who is in heaven meets His children with great love and speaks with them; and the force and power in the word of God is so great that it stands as the support and energy of the Church, the strength of faith for her sons, the food of the soul, the pure and everlasting source of spiritual life."[7]

Openness to God's Word means, first of all, openness of the *understanding*. The Bible is inspired. "Inspired by God and committed once and for all to writing, they impart the word of God Himself without change, and make the voice of the Holy Spirit resound in the words of the prophets and Apostles."[8] God's purposes and thoughts stand always before my own

[6] Vatican Council II, Constitution on the Sacred Liturgy *Sacrosanctum concilium* (December 4, 1963), no. 7.

[7] *DV* 21.

[8] Ibid.

thoughts and sympathies and my misgivings. I do not need constantly to discuss with God or question what he says. "Is it true that God loves me? Can I really be without cares? Are my sins forgiven?" For all eternity it shall be seen that it was right to trust in God's Word. "Heaven and earth will pass away," says Jesus, "but my words will not pass away" (Mt 24:35).

The openness of the understanding also means to read what is written there. We often have the tendency to limit the Bible's message in certain aspects; to read some personal favorite ideas into the biblical texts. But all the texts must be included even when they seemingly contradict each other.

The Bible message is many-dimensioned. Despite the fact that it is infinitely simple in itself, as simple as God, the poverty of human understanding and limitation causes this simplicity to break down into seemingly different opposing elements. Only the one who is prepared to take all these elements without excluding a single one does justice to the Bible. It is enticing to eliminate some difficult elements in order to simplify the synthesis and make the whole thing make sense. Such a simplification falsifies Scripture's Word. The message often sounds paradoxical, bewildering. It must be allowed to do that.

It is difficult for people in our time to believe in and submit themselves to an absolute truth. But only the one who does this has the possibility of receiving God's Word in its fullness.

Openness also concerns *the will*. The message God

proclaims in his Word has a practical character. As a whole, we never find in the Gospel or in the Scriptures theories or speculations. When God communicates a truth, it is always so that we will live it. The ethic of the Gospel can seem hard and unattainable. It is not enough to endure one's enemies, we should love and suffer injustice with patience. It is not easy! But God's Word expresses his will, and this will, if we fulfill it, is the only thing that can make us whole and happy.

The seed, like God's Word, is planted in our hearts and bears fruit in *perseverance* (Lk 8:15). Yes, perseverance. Jesus' commands are so radical that we cannot fulfill them immediately. But if we persevere and do not lose courage, we will be able to do it, or rather it is he who will fulfill his own commands in us.

"Ah! Lord, I know you don't command the impossible", writes Saint Thérèse of Lisieux. "You know better than I do my weakness and imperfection; You know very well that never would I be able to love my Sisters as You love them, unless *You*, O my Jesus, *loved them in me*. It is because You wanted to give me this grace that You made Your *new* commandment. Oh! How I love this new commandment since it gives me the assurance that Your Will is *to love in me* all those You command me to love!"[9] It is with this kind of trust that we may read the "demands" of the Bible.

---

[9] *Story of a Soul: The Autobiography of St. Thérèse of Lisieux*, trans. John Clarke, O.C.D., 3rd ed. (Washington, D.C.: ICS Publications, 1996), p. 221.

Finally, there is also an openness of the heart. A questionable attitude with which we are often confronted in our time is that of constantly doubting the events of the Bible and wondering: "Did that really happen? Did the wise men really come from the East to worship Jesus? When the sick were healed at Bethsaida, did it happen due to a special intervention of God, or should one rather think of mineral springs? If we receive the Bible's statements with the modern mentality of historians, we do not read the Bible, not the Word of God, but human documents. Bible reading is not meaningful if it happens with an objective and distanced attitude that is typical of an observer who has nothing to win or lose. That is what a journalist does who observes an event he will later report. The Bible should be read with the heart.

Is it not strange that we find it difficult to be present to ourselves? We flee from our deepest inner self. Events, news, meetings, our desires, our fear, our work all draw us outward and cause us to lose ourselves, but we can return to our heart, "redire ad cor" (Is 46:8 Vulgate). Yes, it is a question of rediscovering one's heart, as David says (according to the Vulgate) "Your servant has found his heart [invenit servus tuus cor suum] to pray this prayer to you" (2 Sam 7:27). "Oh how it flees this vagabond heart, when we try to come close to God!" sighs Bossuet (1627–1704).

We should not be spectators but actors. God's Word concerns us. God's Words have eternal value; they concern me now. They affect me in this moment. When the priest or the deacon begins the Gospel with "At that time", we can transpose it and understand it as: "At *my* time". Jesus instructs me now, and I may listen to him. The Sermon on the Mount, the Beatitudes, all of this Jesus says *to me* now.

When he says: "you are my friends if you do what I command you" (Jn 15:14), he says it to me. I hear Jesus say to me: "Take heart, my son; your sins are forgiven" (Mt 9:2). It is I who with the scribe say to Jesus: "Teacher, I will follow you wherever you go" (Mt 8:19). And it is I who with the leper say to him: "Lord, if you will, you can make me clean." And it is also I who with joy in my heart hear his answer: "I will; be clean:" (Mt 8:2-3). I am there when the woman anoints Jesus' feet and prays for forgiveness (Lk 7:38). I stand beneath the Cross with Mary. I am there when the disciples wait for the coming of the Holy Spirit.

"Let us bear the Cross and Resurrection, let us bear Bethlehem *within* us . . .", says Saint Jerome (ca. 335-ca. 420). To read about Jesus' birth in Bethlehem is not only a reminder of a historical event. The decisive thing is that Jesus is born in me today.

May Christ be born a thousand times in Bethlehem, but if he is not born in your heart, "death [will] surely be your fate."[10]

If we read with the heart, we will also discover God's

---

[10] Angelus Silesius, *The Cherubinic Wanderer*, trans. Maria Shrady, Classics of Western Spirituality (Mahwah, N.J.: Paulist Press, 1986), p. 76.

heart in his Word. To read the Bible, and above all the
New Testament, this becomes literally *coeur à coeur* with
God, a meeting between the heart of man and God.

Afterward, to the degree that we are faithful in reading the Bible, we become conscious that we have spiritual senses, mainly a spiritual sense of taste that becomes more and more refined. God's Word becomes
ever more "desirable" and gives us a deep joy; we experience it as substantial food. Like the disciples on
the way to Emmaus, we feel that we have a heart and
that it can be burning (Lk 24:32).

If we read the Bible in the spirit in which it was written, we will find more and more how certain words
suddenly appear in a new light. The day dawns, and the
morning star rises in our hearts (2 Pet 1:19). "God's
Word", says Saint Gregory, "is a melody in the night
[carmen in nocte]."

Little by little, we are able to experience that the
Spirit allows us to find and understand just what we
need for the moment. Many also feel less and less need
for other books; perhaps when we are in need, it is only
for the Bible. Saint Therese writes "In this helpless-
ness [during prayer], Holy Scripture and the Imitation
come to my aid; in them I discover a solid and very
pure nourishment. But it is especially the *Gospels* that
sustain me during my hours of prayer, for in them I
find what is necessary for my poor little soul. I am
constantly discovering in them new lights, hidden and
mysterious meanings."[11]

---

[11] *Story of a Soul*, p. 179.

To Become a Reflection of the Scriptures

The Christian tradition has always read the Bible on three levels at the same time. What is said about Israel can be applied to the Church and to me personally. The Word concerns me, my destiny, my life. I am involved. That is how it ought to be. Can I say about my Bible reading what we read in Isaiah: "For as the rain and the snow come down from heaven, and do not return there but water the earth, making it bring forth and sprout . . . so shall my word be that goes forth from my mouth; it shall not return to me empty, but it shall accomplish that which I intend, and prosper in the thing for which I sent it" (55:10–11).

Does God's Word accomplish in me what he wills?

Has it never ever happened to you that after the death of a beloved and appreciated friend or relative's death, in your reading of Scripture you are surprised by a text that could stand as a motto for his life, a text that was exactly suitable for the deceased, that expressed precisely who he was?

Is it not the task of all of us to become a reflection of Scripture, to reflect God's Word in our lives and let it become a concrete and experienced reality?

That is how Mary was a clear mirror in which the Sermon on the Mount and the Beatitudes, indeed, the whole of Scripture became a reality. We have an ability to give life to the Scriptures and, like Mary, to let the Word become flesh, to prepare a body for it.

If we have a deep longing for such an incarnation of

the Word in our lives, we will also read God's Word often, often, often. Bible reading is then, not a pious practice, but rather a need, a necessity of life, just as eating is a necessity of life and not a practice.

And as it not only has to do with eating but also with digesting what we have eaten, so we can also give ourselves the opportunity to digest the word. We cannot digest a long Bible text at once, but we can also perhaps try to live a week or two with a word from Scripture, let that word resound in our lives in all of our encounters, in everything we do and experience. "Your word is a lamp to my feet and a light to my path" (Ps 119:105). Yes, such a word enlightens and leads me; it gives me new hope and new strength.

Something must happen in a person when time and time again he repeats for himself or lets God repeat for him: "Look up and raise your heads, because your redemption is drawing near" (Lk 21:28). Or when he hears God say: "Fear not, for I have redeemed you; I have called you by name, you are mine" (Is 43:1), or this simple, unpretentious verse from the Psalms: "He brought me forth into a broad place" (18:19).

If we usually read Scripture in its entirety, there is no risk that such a word will become isolated or lead to one-sidedness. That single word stands for the whole Word of God and represents all of Scripture. It is like an entryway into the wholeness.

In one single aspect, one single detail, everything can be present.

The history of the Church is in large part God's history. How many religious orders have come into being because a founder or foundress one day was taken by a word from Scripture, was transformed by it, began a new life, and drew many others into this new life.

On February 24, 1209, Saint Francis of Assisi heard the reading during Mass: "Take nothing for your journey, no staff, nor bag, nor bread, nor money; and do not have two tunics" (Lk 9:3), and the Franciscan Order began.

Charles de Foucauld was especially taken by this passage: "And he went down with them and came to Nazareth, and was obedient to them" (Lk 2:51), and new religious families and a new spirituality were born. But it is always so that in that single word the whole is present, seen from a specific perspective.

To Hear the Silence in the Word

"It is better", writes Saint Ignatius of Antioch (d. ca. 110) "with one who remains silent and is someone than with one who speaks and is no one. It is a good thing to instruct, if the one who speaks also acts. One is the Teacher who spoke and it came to be. That which he did in silence is worthy of the Father. The one who truly has Jesus' Word can also hear his silence. In this way he becomes perfect, acts according to what he says, and is recognized in his silence."[12] A person who lives in familiar contact with God's Word

---

[12] *Letter to the Ephesians*, no. 15.

can also listen to God's stillness. The words lead him into an ocean of silence. God is greater than what human language can say about him. The one who reads Scripture in the spirit in which it is written, in the Holy Spirit, receives a growing need for prayer, contemplation, worship. Only there, in silence, can the wonder flow out into God's infinity. There are moments when the Word and the words say to us as to Saint Mary Magdalene "Do not hold me" (Jn 20:17), let go, drown in God's immeasurable ocean.

In the well-known prayer of Saint Elizabeth of the Trinity (1880–1906), we meet both the Word and the silence, listen to God's Word and drown in his silence. She writes: "O Eternal Word, Word of my God, I want to spend my life in listening to You, to become wholly teachable that I may learn all from You." But she also writes: "O my Three, my All, my Beatitude, infinite Solitude, Immensity in which I lose myself, I surrender myself to You as Your prey. Bury Yourself in me that I may bury myself in You until I depart to contemplate in Your light the abyss of Your greatness." [13]

Stillness and silence are both a preparation that is followed by God's presence. "Let all the earth keep silence before him", says Habakkuk (2:20), and Zephaniah: "Be silent before the Lord GOD! For the day of the LORD is at hand" (1:7). "Be silent, all flesh, before

[13] Elizabeth of the Trinity, "O My God, Trinity Whom I Adore", in *The Complete Works*, vol. 1, *General Introduction, Major Spiritual Writings*, trans. Sister Aletheia Kane, O.C.D. (Washington, D.C.: ICS Publications, 1984), pp. 183–84.

the LORD; for he has roused himself from his holy dwelling'' (Zech 2:13). The silence that is a preparation for God's visitation is something we should create ourselves, but it is completely different when the silence is created by God! What he does truly has a different weight.

It has to do with the silence of which the Book of Revelation speaks when it describes how the Lamb in heaven opens the scroll, breaks its seal, and reveals God's secret decision. ''When the Lamb opened the seventh seal, there was silence in heaven for about half an hour'' (8:1).

One can read about this silence in the writing of the mystics. This silence does not deny the Word; instead, it shows the Word's power. Like a rocket launches the spacecraft and shoots it out of the earth's field of gravity into endless space, so also the Word can shoot the person out of the narrow limits of human language into God's infinity.

Epilogue

"As for knowledge, it will pass away. For our knowledge is imperfect. . . . But when the perfect comes, the imperfect will pass away" (1 Corinthians 13:8–10).

It is meaningful and fruitful to have knowledge of God's Word. But in itself, this knowledge is something extremely limited, and it loses its meaning if it is not directed to give way when the perfect comes. The perfect is the encounter with God himself in the Word, far beyond or better said and infinitely closer than all our thoughts and concepts.

In the Word is life, and the life is the light of men (Jn 1:4). God's Word communicates what it is in itself. Overflowing and eternal life. If we wish to seek this life, the Word is there in all its power, constantly at our disposal; our openness to listen and obey decides to what degree it can reach us.

Our rational understanding and our intellectual capacity should become more and more silent in our encounter with the Word. It is our deep intuition, our heart, and our conscience that will be the receiver. If we are sincerely prepared to say Yes to God, we will continually find guidance and strength in his Word.

Not so that we receive our own store from which we can take, but so that we can just take the next step and so that we are constantly assured of his faithful presence in our lives.

We may not content ourselves with crumbs from the table God sets for us in his Word.

"Open your mouth wide," he says, "and I will fill it" (Ps 81:10).